e-Technology and the Fourth Economy

Managerial Communication Series

By: **Carolyn A. Boulger**
University of Notre Dame

Series Editor: **James S. O'Rourke, IV**
University of Notre Dame

THOMSON
™
SOUTH-WESTERN

Australia · Canada · Mexico · Singapore · Spain · United Kingdom · United States

To my family:
Pam, Colleen, Molly, and Kathleen.
And to my colleagues:
Carolyn, Sandra, Cynthia, and Renee.
Thanks.
JSO'R, IV

To my mother, Mary A. Boulger, with love and gratitude for her unconditional support and guidance.
To Lisa Gollan and Bronwyn Clee, Matt Boulger, Joseph Kosek,
and Michele Sexton for their research efforts with this project.
CAB

THOMSON

SOUTH-WESTERN

e-Technology and the Fourth Economy, Managerial Communication Series
James S. O'Rourke, IV, series editor; Carolyn A. Boulger, author

Editor-in-Chief: Jack Calhoun	**Production Editor:** Robert Dreas	**Design Project Manager:** Michelle Kunkler
VP/Team Leader: Melissa Acuña	**Manufacturing Coordinator:** Diane Lohman	**Cover and Internal Designer:** Robb and Associates
Acquisitions Editor: Jennifer Codner	**Compositor:** Lachina Publishing Services	**Cover /Illustration:** © Artville/Richard Cook
Developmental Editor: Taney Wilkins	**Printer:** Transcontinental Printing, Inc. Louiseville, Quebec	
Marketing Manager: Larry Qualls		

Library of Congress
Control Number:
2002109057

ISBN: 0-324-15255-8

AUTHOR BIOGRAPHIES

James Scofield O'Rourke, IV, is director of the Eugene D. Fanning Center for Business Communication at the University of Notre Dame, where he teaches writing and speaking. In a thirty-five year career, he has earned an international reputation in business and corporate communication. *Business Week* magazine again named him one of the "outstanding faculty" in Notre Dame's Mendoza College of Business. Professor O'Rourke has held faculty appointments in such schools as the United States Air Force Academy, the Defense Information School, the United States Air War College, and the Communication Institute of Ireland. He is a regular consultant to Fortune 500 and mid-size businesses, and is widely published in both professional journals and the popular press.

Carolyn A. Boulger, Ph.D., is an Associate Professor of Business and Concurrent Associate Professional Specialist of Management in the Eugene Fanning Center for Business Communication at the University of Notre Dame. She is responsible for teaching Business and Management Communication courses on the undergraduate and graduate levels, as well as electives in "Writing and Presenting a Business Plan," "Management Communication: Technology and the New Economy," "Strategic Communication for Not-for-Profit Organizations," and "Crisis Management." She also serves as an advisor to the Gigot Center for Entrepreneurial Studies, where she coaches MBA teams in the annual Business Plan competition. She earned her Ph.D. in Telecommunications, Journalism, and Advertising from Michigan State University in 1993; her Masters Degree in Journalism from Columbia University in 1985, and her Bachelors Degree from Simmons College in 1984.

TABLE OF CONTENTS

FOREWORD

In recent years, for a variety of reasons, communication has grown increasingly complex. The issues that seemed so straightforward, so simple not long ago are now somehow different, more complicated. Has the process changed? Have the elements of communication, or the barriers to success been altered? What's different now? Why has this all gotten more difficult?

Several issues are at work here, not the least of which is pacing. Information, images, events, and human activity all move at a much faster pace than they did just a decade ago. The most popular, hip new business magazine is named *Fast Company*. Readers are reminded that it's not just a matter of tempo, but a new way of living we're experiencing.

Technology has changed things, as well. We're now able to communicate with almost anyone, almost anywhere, 24/7 with very little effort and very little professional assistance. It's all possible because of cellular telephone technology, digital imaging, the Internet, fiber optics, global positioning satellites, teleconferencing codecs, high-speed data processing, online data storage and . . . well, the list goes on and on. What's new this morning will be old hat by lunch.

Culture has intervened in our lives in some important ways. Very few parts of the world are inaccessible any more. Other people's beliefs, practices, perspectives, and possessions are as familiar to us as our own. And for many of us, we're only now coming to grips with the idea that our own beliefs aren't shared by everyone and that culture is hardly value-neutral.

For a thousand reasons, we've become more emotionally accessible and vulnerable than ever before. You may blame Oprah or Jerry Springer for public outpouring of emotions, but they're not really the cause—they're simply another venue for joy, rage, or grief. The spectacle of thousands of people in London mourning at the death of Diana, Princess of Wales, took many of us in the U.S. by surprise. By the time the World Trade Center towers came down in a terrorist attack, few of us had tears left to give. Who could not be moved by images of those firefighters, laboring in the night, hoping against hope to find a soul still alive in the rubble?

The nature of the world in which we live—one that's wired, connected, mobile, fast-paced, iconically visual, and far less driven by logic—has changed in some not-so-subtle ways in recent days. The organizations which employ us and the businesses which depend on our skills now recognize that communication is at the center of what it means to be successful. And at the heart of what it means to be human.

To operate profitably means that business must now conduct itself in responsible ways, keenly attuned to the needs and interests of it stakeholders. And, more than ever, the communication skills and capabilities we bring to the workplace are essential to our success, both at the individual and at the societal level.

So, what does that mean to you as a prospective manager or executive-in-training? For one thing, it means that communication will involve more than simple writing, speaking, and listening skills. It will involve new contexts, new applications, and new technologies. Much of what will affect the balance of your lives has yet to be invented. But when it is, you'll have to learn to live with it and make it work on your behalf.

The book you've just opened is the second in a series of six that will help you to do all of those things and more. It's direct, simple, and very compact. The aim of my colleague, Professor Carolyn Boulger, is not to provide you with a broad-based education in either business or communication, but rather to pinpoint the issues and ideas most closely associated with successful communication in *e-Technology and the Fourth Economy.*

In a previous volume, Professor Bonnie Yarbrough examined issues related to *Leading Groups and Teams.* She reviews the latest research on small group and team interaction and offers practical advice on project management, intra-team conflict, and improving results. In the volumes that follow, Professor Sandra Collins, a social psychologist by training, will explore *Communication in a Virtual Organization.* The conceptual framework she brings to the discussion will help you to understand how time and distance compression have altered work habits and collaboration. With the help of corporate communication executives and consultants she will show us exciting, current examples of global companies and local groups that illustrate the ways in which our work and lives have permanently changed.

For the iconically challenged (I am one who thinks in words and phrases, not pictures), Graphic Arts Professor Robert Sedlack and Communication Professor Cynthia Maciejczyk will explore *Graphics and Visual Communication for Managers.* If you've ever wondered how to transform words and numbers into pictures, she can help. And for all of us who've ever tried to explain complex issues without success, either aloud or on paper, the message is simple: if you can't say it in a clear, compelling way, perhaps you can show them.

Professor Collins will also examine *Managing Conflict and Workplace Relationships* in a volume that may have more of a lasting impact on how (and with whom) we can work than any of the other titles. Her approach involves far more than dispute resolution or figuring out how limited resources can be distributed equitably among people who think they all deserve more. She shows us how to manage our own emotions, as well as those of others. Creative conflict, along with harmony and synchronicity in the workplace are issues too many of us have avoided because we simply didn't understand them or didn't know what to say.

Finally, Professor Yarbrough will examine *International and Intercultural Communication,* looking both broadly and specifically at issues and opportunities that will seem increasingly important as the business world shrinks and grows more interdependent. As time zones blur and fewer restrictions are imposed on the global movement of capital, raw materials, finished goods, and human labor, people will cling fiercely to the ways in which they were enculturated as youngsters. Culture will become a defining characteristic, not only of peoples and nations, but of organizations and industries.

This is an interesting, exciting, and highly practical series of books. They're small, of course, intended not as comprehensive texts, but as supplemental readings, or as stand-alone volumes for modular courses or seminars. They're engaging because they've been written by people who are smart, passionate about what they do, and more than happy to share what they know. And I've been happy to edit the series, first, because these writers are all friends and colleagues whom I know and have come to trust. Secondly, I've enjoyed the task because this is really interesting stuff. Read on. There is a lot to learn here, new horizons to explore, and new ways to think about human communication.

James S. O'Rourke, IV
The Eugene D. Fanning Center
Mendoza College of Business
University of Notre Dame
Notre Dame, Indiana

Managerial Communication Series

Editor: James S. O'Rourke, IV

The **Managerial Communication Series** is a series of modules designed to teach students how to communicate and manage in today's competitive environment. Purchase only this module as a supplemental product for your Business Communication, Management, or other Business course, or purchase all six modules, packaged together at a discounted price for full coverage of Managerial Communication.

ISBN: **0-324-15254-X**

This text, written by Bonnie T. Yarbrough, reviews the latest research on small group and team interaction, and offers practical advice on project management, intra-team conflict, and improving results. It contains group and team worksheets, progress reports, and sample reporting instruments, as well as classroom discussion questions and case studies.

ISBN: **0-324-15255-8**

This text, written by Carolyn A. Boulger, offers a radical new view of technology's impact on what the author calls "The Fourth Economy," an economic model based entirely on minds in interaction. Technology's role in helping participants in the radically transformed landscape of the twenty-first century is not limited to the transmission and storage of text and data, but extends to the very ways in which people think about and create value.

ISBN: **0-324-15256-6**

This text, written by Sandra D. Collins, explores the risks and opportunities open to those who work in new alliances, partnerships, and non-traditional business models. A look at both theory and practical application offers students and managers the chance to observe successful organizations in action.

*Contact your local South-Western/
Thomson Learning Representative at
800-423-0563. Or visit the series Web site
at* **http://orourke.swcollege.com** *for more
product information and availability.*

ISBN: **0-324-16178-6**

This text, written by Cynthia S. Maciejczyk and Robert P. Sedlack, Jr., offers some practical and useful advice on how to work with graphics and visuals in reports, briefings, and proposals. It also offers direct instruction on how to integrate graphic aids into spoken presentations and public speeches. If you can't say it or write it clearly, you may be able to show it. Dozens of illustrations, drawings, and graphs are included.

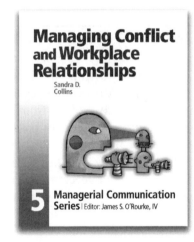

ISBN: **0-324-15257-4**

Learn what social scientists and business executives now know about conflict, personality style, organizational structure, and human interaction. This text, written by Sandra D. Collins, examines the most successful strategies for keeping your edge and keeping your friends. Practical forms, instruments, and applications are included.

ISBN: **0-324-15258-2**

This text, written by Bonnie T. Yarbrough, examines the basis for culture, reviewing the work of social scientists, cultural anthropologists, and global managers on this emerging topic. Definitions of culture, issues of cultural change and how cultures adapt are included, along with practical examples, case studies, and illustrations of how cultural issues are managed both domestically and internationally.

INTRODUCTION

If I have a dollar and you have a dollar, and I give you mine, and you give me yours, what do we have? We each have a dollar, of course. But if I have an idea, and you have an idea, and we give them to each other, what do we have?

COMMUNICATION AS A SOURCE OF ECONOMIC GROWTH IN THE 21ST CENTURY

Communication is positioned to play a key role in the business world of the 21st century—a world with unlimited growth potential. Am I an advocate here for the much-touted new economy? Not really. That term has been poorly defined from the beginning. The new economy has come to be seen, rightly or wrongly, as a quickly passing IT-based fad—more to do with dot.coms than with the real world of business. The new conditions facing the economy and business are more important than that. They have the power to radically challenge old concepts in business and management—and corporate communication. Also, the label new economy somehow implies conflict with the old economy. The new business environment is not in conflict with its predecessors. It is different, yes, but the differences are issues of progress, not of conflict.

If we look back more than a few thousand years, humankind began with an economy based on hunting and gathering. That was the first economy. After that, we settled down and formed the second economy, based on agriculture. By the 17th century, industry created the third economy. Today, we are at the beginning of a change much bigger than a new economy. It is really "The Fourth Economy"—a new era entirely.

THE FOURTH ECONOMY IS DIFFERENT

Wealth in the second economy was defined as the ownership of land and natural resources. To own land was to be rich. And, since the world is finite, the economy was basically a zero-sum game. In the third economy, wealth was created by manufacturing. Being rich was defined as ownership of capital and the means of production. A successful businessman could get richer without necessarily making someone else poorer. In the fourth economy, mind-based resources are the source of wealth. The way to get rich, paradoxically, is by sharing.

In all these transitions, when a new set of conditions arose, leading to a new economy, they did not replace the previous economy. The economics of hunting and gathering still exist in remote areas of the world and among those in the first world who simply love hunting and fishing. We still need food and clothing, metals, petroleum, wood and paper, so the second economy will continue to flourish. There is no sign that we will live anytime soon without cars, trains, houses, or other hardware. The computers of the fourth economy need electric power, so power plants and utility systems are essential. Even with e-mail and e-trade, people and products need to move, so transportation systems and equipment, largely a function of the industrial economy, must be built, maintained, and operated.

Each new phase in the economy not only co-exists with but supports it predecessor, making it more efficient, more productive. Each new economy raises earnings and returns. It creates new wealth, often with the most obvious results in businesses that belong in preceding economies.

Each new economy has made significant contributions to humankind. The second economy provided a certain degree of stability and reliability in basic supplies, such as food and clothing. The machinery of the third economy gave humankind new physical strength and power, as well as added speed to physical prowess. The fourth economy supports mind-based processes and takes them to previously unimaginable levels of strength, power, and speed.

SOURCES AND FORCES DRIVING THE FOURTH ECONOMY

The fourth economy is a set of new conditions for business, economic, social, and human development. It marks a transformation, not only from an industrial to a post-industrial economy, but from an industrial to a post-industrial society.

The sources and forces driving the fourth economy may be found beyond traditional economic boundaries. Our times are characterized by a broad range of dramatic new trends, creating change in virtually all aspects of our lives. Among these trends:

- New sciences and technologies. The fourth economy is high-tech in every sense of the term: Information technology, life sciences, astronomy, nano-physics, new materials, and complexity theory are just a few examples of scientific influence on economic life.
- A cross-national awareness. The fourth economy knows no political or national boundaries, operating in what some have called a World Without Walls.
- A new base for wealth creation. In the fourth economy, growth is built on "minds in interaction," not on the limits of physical resources. The human mind, by contrast, is not a fixed or limited resource, and for the first time in history, the economy has potential for unlimited growth. This changes many of our assumptions about everything from business practices to metrics and benchmarking.
- Multiculturalism. The fourth economy thrives on variety, diversity, multiculturalism, and difference itself as a source of inspiration for "minds in interaction."
- A search for common protocols. The world we're entering now asks not for separate protocols but for commonality of protocols, interoperability, and an increased tolerance for trial-and-error development.

- New concepts of time. In an economy in which time is more valuable than capital, those who have limited amounts must rethink how they plan to use their time.
- New waves of creativity. The changes we're witnessing have the potential to develop into a global win-win economy of unlimited creativity. New ways of thinking and new ways of looking at the world will characterize this transformation.
- New roles of government. The role of governments will not disappear in the fourth economy but will be refocused to provide and support the fundamentals of human security, development, education, health, and investments in mind-based infrastructure.

THE RESULT IS A DIFFERENT WORLD AND A DIFFERENT ECONOMY

Value is increasingly created through mental processes: exchanging ideas. Physical resources play a significantly smaller role in the ongoing value-creation process. When we buy a CD, software, or a cell phone, or when we go to the movies or a theme park, only a small share of what we pay for is physical. We're really paying for mind-based assets. And, chances are that the money we spend has been earned through mind work rather than physical work. More than two-thirds of all working Americans now make their living by processing or moving ideas, less than one-third by moving or processing things.

NEW MANAGEMENT PRIORITIES IN THE FOURTH ECONOMY

Here is a short list of challenges that will influence business management during this century.

1. Unprecedented pace of fast, unpredictable change, has already begun to replace the step-by-step or business as usual patterns of previous economies.

   Alvin Toffler introduced us to the concept of Future Shock in 1970 by comparing our arrival in the economy of the future with that of a traveler who suddenly experiences culture shock on arrival in a new and vastly different society. Percy Barnevik of General Motors says management used to be compared to sailing. Today, he writes, "management is more like whitewater rafting in class E rivers." Colin Powell, in accepting the nomination to become U.S. Secretary of State, said prophetically, "Challenges and crises that we don't know anything about right now will come along."

2. We will uncover new sources of wealth and write new definitions of what creates value. The primary source of wealth today is "minds in interaction."

   The changing emphasis from earth-based and capital-based assets to nonfinancial, mind-based performance and perception value drivers was first signaled as the principal agents of wealth creation by writers such as Peter Drucker in the 1990s. His work was quickly followed by the thinking of Leif Edvinsson and Karl-Erik Sveniby of Sweden; and Frederick Reichheld, Robert Shiller, and Richard Thaler of the United States.

3. Strong and intricate networks of relationships, as well as interdependence among people, companies, and countries are the keys to survival, growth, and earnings.

   The traditional, nonemotional view of the company as an independent legal unit is increasingly replaced by views of the company as a living organism. The crucial dimension is the constant exchange or symbiosis between the company and its environment. As a consequent, no company can be seen or evaluated independently of its context. The most critical factors for a company's success or failure will not be found within the organization itself, but at the boundary lines between the company and its environment—the work site for communication.

THE ROLE OF E-TECHNOLOGY IN THE FOURTH ECONOMY

This dramatic new landscape, in which minds do the heavy lifting and ideas become capital, must have both a means of production and a system of transportation and storage. In the pages that follow, my friend and colleague Carolyn Boulger will describe these phenomena and explain the role of communication in navigating unfamiliar turf. Her work is both innovative and insightful, and remarkably easy to understand. What you have in your hands is her guide to the new world ahead—a world in which innovation, growth, and economic survival will depend on your understanding of human communication.

Hans V. A. Johnsson
Senior Management Consultant
The Kreab Group
Stockholm, Sweden

1 AN OVERVIEW OF E-TECHNOLOGY AND COMMUNICATION

The convergence of communication, technology, and business affects every facet of our lives. In a world where progress is increasingly measured in byte-size packages rather than in mass industrial production, knowledge has become the new form of currency. We trade personal information—our social security number, credit cards, shopping preferences, our own mailing address and those of friends—for the convenience of online transactions. We send e-mails to one another, often oblivious to the fact that they are never private and can never be permanently destroyed. We click through web sites and talk through handles in chat rooms, unaware that our conversations are traceable by those who wish to learn more about us as we seek to learn about them. Welcome to the fourth economy.

In the fourth economy, the currency of knowledge carries with it a hefty interest rate: the loss of personal privacy. There are no rate cuts in sight. Building momentum in tandem are Internet technology growth forecasts, shattering paradigms for how we communicate both in and out of the workplace. Network bandwidth has been growing at a rate of 36 percent per year and is expected to increase to 43 percent in the years just ahead. By 2005, bandwidth will have increased tenfold over 1998 levels.[1]

Consider that before the close of the decade, industry experts such Dr. Tony O'Driscoll, IBM Executive in Residence at North Carolina State University, predict that personal computers could disappear entirely. "Visual information might well be written directly onto our retinas by devices in our eyeglasses or contact lenses," he says. "'Visiting a web site' will mean entering a virtual reality environment. By 2029, we may have billions of nanobots traveling through the capillaries of our brain, communicating directly with our biological neurons. Nanobots could take up positions close to every interneuronal connection coming from all of our biological sensory receptors. When we want to experience nonvirtual reality (that is, the real thing), our nanobots will simply remain still. If we want to return to virtual reality, they can suppress all input coming from our real senses and replace them with the appropriate signals."[2]

Throughout the landscape of global commerce, what has changed is as much a challenge to human communication as it is to communication enhanced through technology. The Internet is not just about e-commerce or web sites. Today's technology affects every department in an organization—marketing, sales, research and development, manufacturing, recruiting, employee retention and benefits, investor relations, distribution chains, and more—as well as customer and market communications. We now have more channel choices through which to communicate than at any point in history, and more ways to replace face-to-face communication, if we so choose. Never has it been so easy for us to be out of the communication loop. It will be imperative, then, that management communication foster connectedness rather than create workplace isolation.

THE PURPOSE OF THIS BOOK

For those who will work in management communication, this book examines five areas of technology that are essential to the fourth economy:

1. Communicating with e-technology tools,
2. Learning through e-technology,
3. Working virtually,
4. Evaluating e-technology in the workplace, and
5. Assessing e-mail and web policies and usage.

To begin the transformation to integrated communications, businesses and large organizations must train their people to recognize appropriate channels for communication within and among various audience groups. "Having a business-literate organization in the fourth economy means having employees who can actively participate in bringing value to the organization," says K. Berman.[3] They can do this only when they know and understand the organization's goals and how their work affects those goals. Employees may be better motivated as they come to understand how they fit into the larger organization." When managers take the time to provide a bigger-picture view to employees, the organization demonstrates trust on the one hand and holds employees accountable for business decisions on the other.

Tech Talk ▼

"The productivity growth seen in recent years likely represents the benefits of the ongoing diffusion and implementation of a succession of technological advances."

— Alan Greenspan, Chairman,
U.S. Federal Reserve, June 1999 ▲

For many managers, creating this trust means letting go of supervisory responsibilities that were once central to their own job descriptions. Within many industries, managers must now grapple with the reality that what was their dominant area of expertise at one time is now a general expectation of the workforce. Consider how increasingly

- Intellectual work is replacing physical work,
- Employees work more independently in knowledge production roles rather than being told specifically what to do,
- More responsibility for determining how projects are accomplished is now placed on individual employees,
- Advanced education and solid resumes are stronger indicators of success than physical strength or family connections, and
- Flexible work hours from remote locations have replaced the typical eight-hour shift.[4]

What is certain for managers is that access to e-technology has created a whole new realm for business communication. Michael Schrage, Merrill Lynch Forum Fellow, Director for the Forum's Innovation Grant Competition, and research associate at the M.I.T. Media Lab, writes: "Gone are the days when internal memoranda circulated in hardcopy throughout the office via mail trays. Meetings that were held regularly and lasted for hours are now held on an as-needed basis using tele- or video-conferencing facilities."[5] Employees communicate much more frequently today with their supervisors, peers, and customers because technology, including e-mail, fax machines, cellular phones, and wireless handheld devices, is so much easier to use.

In this new age, experts overwhelmingly believe technology has strengthened relationships with co-workers. Schrage says that the real value of a medium lies more in the communities it creates than in the information it carries.[6] These communities allow people to communicate in new ways, which they have quickly come to crave.

"Along every meaningful dimension, these technologies permit individuals and institutions alike to sculpt new facets of interaction," says Schrage. "Intimacy, anonymity, trust, openness, access, passion, negotiation, hierarchy, coordination, and collaboration can all be meditated, monitored, and managed via networks ostensibly designed to carry bits.

Certainly, different generations have different views about what the most important technological developments of the past 20 years have been. Survey respondents in a Merrill Lynch study identified the one change that they believe has had the greatest impact on their life personally (from personal home computers, laptop computers, beepers, cell phones, fax machines, remote controls, cable TV, VCRs, the Internet, or any other technology change). Figure 1-1 shows that more than half of the Generation X population surveyed indicated that computers

Figure 1-1   What Technological Change Has Had the Greatest Personal Impact?

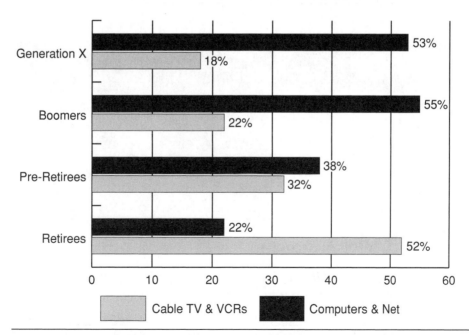

Source: M. Schrage. "The Relationship Revolution." The Merrill Lynch Forum. Retrieved July 20, 2001, from *http://www.ml.com/woml/forum/relation.htm.*

and the 'Net had the greatest single influence, while a comparable population of retirees answered to the same degree regarding the advent of cable TV and VCRs.[7]

Tech Talk ▼

"There are two fundamental equalizers in life—the Internet and education."
— John Chambers, CEO
Cisco Systems, 1999 ▲

Merrill Lynch commissioned a public-opinion survey by The Luntz Research Companies in 1997 to accompany Michael Schrage's analysis (Figure 1-1). The Luntz Research Companies interviewed 800 American adults and an oversample of 200 computer specialists—defined as individuals who either work in the computer industry or extensively use computer networks or software in the course of their jobs on a daily basis. The overall margin of error for the survey is ±3.5 percent.

As Schrage points out by referring to this survey in the Merrill Lynch Forum, many Americans have been slow to recognize the impact of these technical developments in the workplace and on the communication that they help to facilitate there. When asked "Have computers, computer networks, and e-mail greatly strengthened, somewhat strengthened, somewhat weakened, or greatly weakened your relationships with the people you work with?" most non-technology experts were skeptical of the perceived impact of technology on relationships with office peers (see Figure 1-2).[8]

How people see and think about workplace relationships and the communication that takes place within them is mixed, as is the range of reactions from many managers. For example, if

Figure 1-2   Has Technology Strengthened Relationships with Co-Workers?

	Technology Experts	Adult Americans
Total Strengthened	72%	40%
Greatly	35%	14%
Somewhat	37%	26%
Total Weakened	5%	7%
Greatly	1%	1%
Somewhat	4%	6%
Does Not Apply	24%	51%

Note: Sample for this question includes 191 experts and 573 adult Americans who report they are currently working.

Source: M. Schrage. "The Relationship Revolution." The Merrill Lynch Forum. Retrieved July 15, 2001, from *http://www.ml.com/woml/forum/relation.htm*.

some employees maintain personal homepages while others do not, what are the new rules regarding interpersonal relationships? If it is faster and easier to send e-mail messages, will employees bother to walk down the hall for personal interaction with colleagues? And if web-tracking software can monitor the web sites visited and e-mails sent—allowing electronic surveillance to substitute for personal trust—what ethical messages does an organization communicate with its employees?

> **Tech Talk ▼**
>
> *"The new electronic interdependence recreates the world in the image of a global village."*
> — Marshall McLuhan, *The Gutenberg Galaxy* (London: Routledge & Kegan Paul, 1962, p. 31) ▲

In short, how have the playing field and the rules for communication changed within workplace relationships, especially those that are driven or influenced by technology? That's the one question that this book hopes to answer. While issues of privacy, law, and ethics also intersect with communication and technology, those areas are specifically outside the scope of this text. Rather, technology choices and their uses within management communication comprise the backdrop for this book.

ANOTHER PERSPECTIVE ON HOW TECHNOLOGY IS AFFECTING US

One point of view on how to navigate technically enhanced communication is that of *Wired Digital* writers John Browning and Spencer Reiss. They offer these thoughts as a preface to their "Encyclopedia for the New Economy," in which they argue that neither managers nor employees know how to measure, compete in, or oversee productivity in this new economy:

> **Tech Talk ▼**
>
> In 2001, nearly 14 million U.S. employees using e-mail or the Internet were continuously monitored by their employers.
> — According to a study released by the Privacy Foundation in July 2001 ▲

"The fact that Bill Gates is the world's richest man belies a huge shift in the values of capitalism. Microsoft has annual sales of US $11 billion, and most of its assets walk in and out of its doors wearing T-shirts. Yet the stock market values the company at well over $150 billion—far more than either IBM (sales $76 billion, market cap $100 billion) or General Motors (sales $160 billion, market cap $50 billion). Why? Because the rules of competition are changing to favor companies like Microsoft over paragons of the industrial age.

Microsoft's rise is a testimony to the power of ideas in the new economy. Working with information is very different from working with steel and glass from which our grandparents built their wealth. Information is easier to produce and harder to control than stuff you can drop on your foot. For a start, computers can copy it and ship it anywhere, almost instantly and almost for free. Production and distribution, the basis of industrial power, can increasingly be taken for granted. Innovation and marketing are all.

What's true is that the shift to an information economy is redefining how we need to think about both good times and bad. We don't know how to measure this new economy, because the productivity of a decision maker is harder to grasp than the productivity of someone bolting together cars. We don't know how to manage its companies, because decision makers can't be told what to do. We don't know how to compete in it, because information seeps so easily that supermarkets now offer banking services and Amazon.com has infiltrated its virtual bookshelves into web sites the world over.

Tech Talk ▼

Cyber-loafing accounts for 30 to 40 percent of lost worker productivity every day.
— According to the International Data Corp (IDC) of Framingham, Mass. ▲

We don't know how to oversee it, or whether it ultimately needs oversight at all.

A final thing we don't know is where—or how—the revolution will end. We are building it together, all of us, by the sum of our collective choices." [9]

Never have more choices for communication and technology presented themselves to managers and business owners. From this new technology arises new questions that managers must answer each day:

- Should employees be allowed to work regularly from home?
- If employees work with company-owned hardware such as laptops or cell phones, is personal use ever acceptable?
- Which employees should have access to e-mail and web use? How should their use of these tools be monitored, if at all?
- When are face-to-face meetings really necessary? If necessary, how often should they occur?
- When are printed documents really necessary, as opposed to electronic ones?
- Does an investment in communications technology really enhance productivity? Where is the ceiling above which the cost of technology exceeds the extra value it brings?
- Does communication technology enhance or hinder connectedness in the workplace?

THE ROAD AHEAD FOR MANAGEMENT COMMUNICATION

Networked conversations between individuals, teams, companies, and markets are allowing the emergence of new forms of knowledge exchange and social organization. Industry observers such as Jay Cross of the Internet Time Group note that "markets are smarter, less loyal, more fickle, highly demanding, and not afraid to talk about it to anyone willing to listen." [10]

Cross notes that today, the company's organizational chart is hyperlinked, not hierarchical, meaning that respect for hands-on knowledge wins over respect for abstract authority.

He also points out that it is far more difficult to keep secrets than at any time in our country's history. News, both good and bad, can spread in seconds, allowing networked markets to sometimes know more than individual companies do about their own products. Likewise, this continuous networked conversation tends to outshine the predictability of printed documents, with stakeholders and other observers more likely to hit the company web sites than read annual reports. Because markets are now networked person to person, the flow of information has ceased to be a direct

Tech Talk ▼

Nearly 70 percent of members polled by the American Management Association have written policies in place regarding use of company e-mail.
— The American Management Association, December 2000 ▲

and impenetrable public relations funnel though which one-way messages travel safely and intact. Cross adds that as a result, "stakeholder groups are no longer based on relationships built to last. Rather, employees and shareholders can now reposition their interests—both professional and financial—in a time-span measured in mouse clicks."[11]

In the fourth economy, work communities within which communication occurs are not defined by the physical confines of walls or offices. Rather, they are based on a desire to communicate in real time, anytime, from anywhere, to anyone. In this conversation, there is no opt-out policy for managers of communication.

Inside companies, employees also talk with each other through the traditional grapevines and their electronic counterparts: corporate intranets, Listservs, e-mail, bulletin boards, and project management applications. These conversations concern much more than human resource policies or profitability. The management communication tightrope attempts to control some content yet, at the same time, offer access to a widening pool of information to further strengthen a knowledge-enhanced workforce. Managers peripherally involved in the process passively write policies for handing the currency of information, while those who are genuinely committed take a different approach by viewing the greatest value of knowledge—whether raw ideas, criticism, or intellectual discourse—in *how* it is shared and *that* it is shared.

WHERE THIS BOOK WILL TAKE YOU

In the next five chapters, we'll examine the balance of workplace relationships, management communication, electronic technology, interpersonal and interoffice discourse, and channel choices and consequences. The discussion is twofold: both a presentation of issues at the convergence of communication, technology, and business; and an overview of options for managers making choices concerning communication in the workplace. Let's take a look at these options and issues.

COMMUNICATING WITH E-TECHNOLOGY TOOLS

A range of e-technology tools supports both individual and team collaboration and learning. Those charged with deciding which tools to offer their employees will need to appreciate the benefits and drawbacks that each option offers.

For example, Chapter 2 will explain how an intranet differs from a corporate portal, the value of requiring instant messaging access for all employees, teleconferencing versus business travel, wireless options and capabilities, and tools to help support remote teams and their projects.

ISSUES IN THE CHANGING MODE OF COMMUNICATION: ONLINE WORKPLACE BEHAVIORS AND THE POLICIES THAT GUIDE THEM

Chapter 3 examines online workplace behaviors such as e-mail use and web surfing, which present serious value conflicts for managers. On the one hand, e-mail is a highly efficient tool for sharing information and documents rapidly and efficiently. Yet the need to monitor e-mail and web site usage for inappropriate content—from racist or sexist jokes or comments to personal threats or trade secrets—raises concerns for employee privacy. Some employees may be reluctant to embrace e-technology entirely, while others may rely on it exclusively at the expense of more traditional and often more appropriate formats.

Tech Talk ▼

On most pornographic web sites, up to 70 percent of traffic takes place during work hours.
— According to SexTracker, a service that monitors usage of such sites ▲

FOCUS ON E-LEARNING: WHO EXACTLY ARE E-LEARNERS?

Who exactly are e-learners? In Chapter 4, we'll provide some definitions of e-learning and distinguish between the ways the concept is used in corporate and educational settings. We'll look at the benefits it offers to virtual workers, managers, human resource personnel, and the larger organization. You'll have an opportunity to review the various types of e-learning tools and environments and see what factors affect success rates across current e-learning options.

We discuss how the e-learning process is best managed, focusing on how to implement an e-learning environment, how to develop an e-learning program, and how to select technology for your e-learning goals. We'll conclude by looking at ways to optimize your investment in e-learning so that dropout rates are manageable.

FOCUS ON WORKING VIRTUALLY: WHAT ARE VIRTUAL TEAMS?

What is virtual work, and what communication factors influence the success of such work? Chapter 5 explores how the communication function changes with and within virtual teams and describes how to anticipate both where and how communication challenges may arise beforehand.

Developing a communication strategy for the team can help to prevent many communication problems and adds structure and predictability to a team, allowing them to work with more confidence. Another section includes suggestions for team leaders to make sure inter-team communication stays on course.

EVALUATING E-TECHNOLOGY IN THE WORKPLACE: MEASURING THE VALUE OF E-TECHNOLOGY IN THE WORKPLACE

Measuring success brings closure to any process, communication notwithstanding. In Chapter 6, we'll introduce you to some tools that will help you determine what gains technology has delivered to your organization and at what expense. We'll also look at feedback and evaluation tools for employees who will live and work in technologically enhanced communication environments.

DISCUSSION QUESTIONS

1. What does having a business-literate organization in the fourth economy mean to managers of corporate communication and the employees who work for them?

2. According to Merrill Lynch, how does age effect people's beliefs regarding the significance of new technology?

3. How do *Wired Digital* writers John Browning and Spencer Reiss describe the new economy?

4. How do many non-technology experts perceive the impact of technology on relationships with office peers?

5. How has the layout of the typical company organizational chart changed in the fourth economy?

ENDNOTES

1. "Business Process Revolution." Retrieved August 1, 2001, from *http://www.iec.org/online/tutorials/bus_proc/topic01.html*.

2. T. O'Driscoll. "Push, Pull, Connect, Ignore: What Is the Optimal e-Learning Strategy?" Training Directors' Forum, June 10–13, 2001, Las Vegas, Nevada. Citing *Business 2.0,* September 26, 2000, p. 163.

3. "Business Literacy: Training that transforms Employees into Business People." Berman, K. (2001). Training Directors' Forum, June 10–13, Las Vegas, Nevada.

4. O'Driscoll, op.cit.

5. M. Schrage. "The Relationship Revolution." The Merrill Lynch Forum. Retrieved July 15, 2001, from *http://www.ml.com/woml/forum/relation.htm*.

6. Ibid.

7. Ibid.

8. Ibid.

9. J. Browning and S. Reiss. "Encyclopedia for the New Economy." *Wired Digital*. Retrieved June 19, 2001, from *http://hotwired.lycos.com/special/enel*.

10. J. Cross. "Research on the Future of Learning and Business." InternetTime Group, Berkeley, Calif. Retrieved June 20, 2001, from *http://www.internettime.com*.

11. Ibid.

2 COMMUNICATING WITH E-TECHNOLOGY TOOLS

People generally see change as threatening, painful, and exhausting. Only 20 percent of those who work in organizations embrace change and thrive on it, while some 50 percent go with the flow. About 30 percent actively resist change or deliberately try to make new initiatives fail. This means that 80 percent of the workforce must be "pulled along" when asked to make changes, or embrace new technology.[1]

Even though e-technology has the ability to enhance communication, it also can easily hamper efforts. So, as we create new environments and channels for electronic communication, it's important to understand the technical options, obstacles, and opportunities inherent in each choice. This is especially true when the technology will support training of a delicate nature, such as handling matters concerning appropriate workplace behaviors.

In this chapter, we'll examine how mangers can gain commitment, or buy-in, by employees when introducing new technology to foster communication vital to the success in everything from teamwork to training. This chapter also reviews the different technologies managers have to choose from as they make changes within physical and virtual workspaces.

Tech Talk ▼

"The more complex the technology, the faster people will log off."
— Jessica Lipnack,
    virtual teaming expert ▲

THE ELECTRONIC PATH OF LEAST RESISTANCE

Sometimes managers have to market new technology to those employees who may be cynical or simply reluctant. In the Executive MBA program at the University of Notre Dame, Director of Technology Bill Brewster deals regularly with managers intimidated by technology.

"If they've had a bad experience with technology before, they're likely to believe that all experiences will be similar," explains Brewster. "So it's really important to make sure that when people face new technology there is someone qualified available to both train and answer questions."[2]

Like any customer, it's up to the manager/trainer to uncover the needs of her employees and match those needs with a solution. That is, you must implement a strategy that communicates the value of technology to the employee. In general, this process includes the following steps:

- **Recognize that learning curves vary widely.** Don't allow early adopters to drive the pace of employee training. Remember that reluctant users are least likely to ask questions but most likely to question the need for new technology. Demonstrating how technology can make some tasks easier, more efficient, and faster will help improve buy-in rates from the less than enthused employees.

- **Anticipate questions and offer answers** to employees long before the information is needed. Also recognize that some learners lean toward logical, factual answers, while others prefer anecdotes and real-world success stories.

- **Whenever possible, show and tell.** Recognize that the majority of learners are more likely to retain information when they both see the process and hear the explanation of how the process works.

- **Develop interactive support for training** to allow employees to get help when and where they need it. This may be as simple as a pop-up help window, or a combination of computer-based and human support. Many employees would rather pick up the telephone and call a colleague for assistance than sift through an online manual or web tutorial.

- **Communicate with departmental supervisors** by sending them short e-mail messages that clearly outline the value of e-technology initiatives for the organization (and for them). Share cross-departmental success stories and praise progress made toward departmental goals for technology implementation, training, and usage.

- **Replace fear with contagious excitement** by creating incentives for those involved in the training process. For example, reward employees who master use of the corporate portal by letting them work from home occasionally.

- **Keep all training interactive** by communicating with employees openly before, during, and after the process. Employees are less likely to give up on new technology if they know that a friendly colleague is available to help through the learning transitions.

- **Ensure credibility by anticipating how the business will accept the technology** and how it will assist in moving communication strategies forward. If the ability to conduct online polls, for example, could provide current and relevant data for ongoing projects, employees may be more motivated to become proficient in such software.

Tech Talk ▼

"In the beginning, training was simple. You only needed a classroom, a blackboard, and students."
— Eric R. Parkes, Ph.D., President and CEO, ASK International ▲

Management must acknowledge that even with the most aggressive training, some employees will remain reluctant to use technology to communicate with one another, preferring face-to-face interaction. Of course, in numerous situations, face-to-face communication is most appropriate. Congratulatory or disciplinary messages, for example, are situations requiring more traditional communication channels, whether spoken or written. But it is still important to uncover reasons why some employees resist using technology to communicate.

Understanding the needs of these employees will help managers develop an effective strategy for motivating employees to use e-technology as a communication tool.

One way around reluctant employees is to engage a facilitator, either internally or externally. An internal facilitator could simply be an enthusiastic employee who can influence others to see the benefits of working with new technology. However, if this employee is himself an early adopter, the reluctant user may sense a lack of camaraderie between herself and the facilitator. This has the potential to create interoffice communication problems if facilitators and reluctant employees work together on other tasks. An external facilitator, or representative of the technology developer, is often assigned as an account representative to offer support during the training process. Whether internal or external, facilitators should be able to achieve several outcomes:

Increase awareness and interest among employees by marketing the benefits of using the new technology through specifically designed and scheduled activities.

- Greet people who come into the electronic community and make them feel valuable and welcome.
- Identify other enthusiastic members and enlist their voluntary help to take on roles and formulate other activities that will support the initial goal of getting employees comfortable with the new technology.
- Seek out those who are not participating and inquire about their needs.
- Continuously evaluate progress, particularly where some activities have worked well, and collaborate with the team to develop more effective participation strategies.[3]

E-T PHONE HOME

We know from electronics that the farther you are from the source, the weaker and more distorted the signal. Likewise, the greater the distance from your manager, the greater the effort you both must exert to keep in touch. Despite tremendous advances in electronic communication, there is no one tool that can successfully channel all messages for all audience groups under all circumstances. Bill Bruck, Ph.D., of The Caucus Consortium, explains that conference calls work for team check-ins but are not the best choice for the sustained communication required to accomplish team projects. The

Tech Talk ▼

"When an organization coordinates activities in 180 countries in an attempt to foster economic growth and reduce world poverty, it learns a few things about collaboration."
— Paulie Ramprasad, Manager,
The World Bank ▲

Caucus Consortium provides online collaborative environments for global organizations including CNA, IBM, Hewlett-Packard, and Warner Lambert. He adds that Listservs, or e-mail subgroups based on projects or interest, accommodate one-to-many communication but lack the real-time appeal of discussion software or rich media presentation technology that supports images as clear as we have come to expect on television.[4]

Regardless of communication technology choice, a general rule, then, for managers and facilitators alike is to *increase* the frequency of communication as you *increase* the distance between communicators. Distance may be defined in a geographic or physical capacity or as the unfortunate result of interpersonal relationship problems between managers and employees.

THE RANGE OF E-TECHNOLOGY COMMUNICATION TOOLS

It is dangerous to use a *Field of Dreams* philosophy ("If you build it, they will come") with e-technology communication tools. High adoption rates are driven more by convenience or ease-of-use than the factors of speed or cost of communication. Which collaborative functions are most useful depends, then, on the type of organization and team. For example, an international team dispersed across time zones would not have much use for a chat room or a real-time web-cast presentation. Rather, a threaded discussion board would be more useful, as the threads allow simultaneous and easy access to related messages, documents, and other postings. Similarly, a senior management team would benefit more from a threaded discussion board that tracks strategy and decisions over a long period of time than from a project-management system used on the local level.[5]

THE TELECONFERENCING ALTERNATIVE TO TRAVEL

Satellite teleconferencing is often mistaken for the technology of the future, when in fact it's commonplace in most corporations today. Industry leaders such as Wal-Mart, J. C. Penny, and Ford Motor Company use this technology to train their associates every day. The cost of teleconferencing is almost always much lower than flying a group of distributed people to a meeting site, paying for hotel and meal expenses, and covering any additional expenditures associated with these events.

SO, WHAT IS TELECONFERENCING?

Teleconferencing allows communicators to use a telephone to communicate with anyone, anytime, in a single conversation. Regardless of venue, conference calls tie employees together across time zones and area codes. With teleconferencing, you can:

- Meet on short notice,
- Avoid making repetitive calls to numerous parties,
- Increase your effectiveness by reaching a wider audience,
- Facilitate group discussion and feedback,
- Eliminate traditional global boundaries,
- Improve communication flow within your organization, and
- Speed up the decision-making process.[6]

To ensure success, support for teleconferencing must come from meeting participants. These meetings usually work best if documents are electronically distributed in advance. E-mail is a frequent companion tool to teleconferencing, allowing participants to make changes to documents and instantly share them with each other while participating in the call. In high-stakes teleconferencing cases—those in which the cost of technical failures would be very high—company representatives are often sent to participate in teleconferencing from the other side. This allows information that may initially appear broken and confused during the meeting to be cleared up immediately.[7]

Even though it is collaborative, teleconferencing does not support many advanced functions that require high levels of interaction, such as online white-boarding and real-time document sharing between participants. Task support of this nature requires a combination of collaborative applications and collaborative tools, the former is a process the latter a product. Applications drive the communication transaction, while tools host the forum in which the communication process is transacted and completed. These tools also may be synchronous (same time) such as web casts or live Internet-based training, or asynchronous (different time) such as voice mail or e-mail. Some tools are delivered synchronously and then retained for asynchronous review at a later time. Some examples of collaborative applications include:[8]

- Hosted web conferencing, application sharing, white-boarding of diagrams or slides, and organizational charting. These applications allow conference call participants to view PowerPoint presentations and other applications through a web browser or proprietary graphical interface. State-of-the-art Executive MBA programs accomplish this task through the use of a split T-1 line. Half the line is used for videoconferencing, while the other half allows computer images used in the classroom to be transmitted offsite.
- E-mail and chat functions let groups of colleagues or business partners see who is online and send text messages to each other, either through an intranet or over the Internet.
- Group calendar applications let users coordinate meetings and track other events using a browser or e-mail notification.
- Project management and document management include groupware applications through which co-workers can work together on documents stored on a local database or on a remote server and track changes.

Collaboration tools include the by-products generated through the use of applications like those we've just discussed. They include but are not limited to

- Virtual classes, lectures, or simulations;
- Tutorials or CD-ROMs;
- Scheduled chats or e-mail, and
- Discussion forums or threaded discussion boards.

CORPORATE PORTALS: ONE-STOP INFORMATION OUTSOURCING

Increasingly, collaboration tools are used to provide online workspace for organizations and their employees. These corporate portals provide applications that focus on communication and information. They increase convenience by serving as technology infrastructure that employees may access no matter where they choose to work. Portals enable organizations to unlock both internally and externally stored information and provide users with a single, personalized gateway to credible information they need to make informed business decisions.

The best corporate portals connect employees not only with *everything* they need but also with *everyone* they need. In this sense, a top-notch corporate portal can replace your traditional desktop, just as the computer modem replaces your commute to work. One example of such a product is a software package called CommuniSpace, which uses online images (pictures) of employees to help encourage and improve communication among those connected to a network of their peers. The network means that each individual can share knowledge, make decisions, and solve problems but is never alone. CommuniSpace-supported activities include brainstorming, real-time chatting, and document exchange. Those are just some of the activities supported by all web portals, but this software package personalizes the communication process by allowing users to see still images of each other while writing or chatting.

Tech Talk ▼

"While world population is growing at 6.6 percent annually, the number of web users is increasing by 370 percent annually."

— Tony Driscoll, Ph.D.,
Senior Consultant, IBM e-Business
Strategy and Design ▲

CommuniSpace Chairman and President Eric Vogt explains that there are three types of corporate communities: those focused on developing strategic initiatives, best practices, and innovation; customer-focused groups dedicated to market research; and learning communities focused on orientation and executive education. "To be effective, they all must share a concern or purpose," Vogt says. "They must communicate, build relationships, and develop trust. When people work in CommuniSpace, they can connect with a network of colleagues with whom they need to share knowledge, make decisions, problem solve, and innovate."[9]

In environments such as those offered by CommuniSpace, value creation occurs through knowledge-building. People are connected to processes and resources, rather than simply using different technologies that happen to be part of the same platform.

To achieve true collaboration, connecting people and knowledge work processes is paramount. While any communication that takes place over the Internet occurs through some form of collaborative software tool—each with its unique data-sharing capabilities—it is only through the combination of these tools that their real strengths emerge. That powerful combination, however, comes at a high financial cost, with most systems taking upwards of $1 million to implement. Brewster explains that the high costs are associated with what is required to transmit audio, images, and data via an ISDN or T-1 line. On average, it costs about $120 per hour to run the equipment domestically and about $400 to Western Europe. And it costs $1,000 or more per hour to reach Pacific Rim countries.[10]

Despite slight distinctions in definition, collaborative applications and tools indeed work in tandem to support the electronic communication process. Most people who collaborate electronically don't think much about the equipment involved, yet they rely on them. Rather than getting in a car or onto an airplane, employees stay at their workstations, log in with passwords, and take part in an arranged conference while viewing a PowerPoint presentation or participating in online tutorials.

At the University of Notre Dame, the Mendoza College of Business' Executive MBA (EMBA) program uses collaborative software to enhance both its degree and nondegree programs. Each year, hundreds of students—most of them professional, experienced managers in their mid-30s—enroll in EMBA programs and nondegree programs at Notre Dame, separated by miles but not a desire to learn collaboratively from the resident faculty as well as each other.

"We have students in our programs from New York throughout the Midwest to California," explains Leo Burke, Associate Dean and Director of Executive Education. "They work as study teams, but, since they're not co-located all the time, they can't work face to face. What becomes clear is that for their learning experience to be successful we have to increase their opportunities for interaction."[11]

Burke and his technology team selected a web-based collaboration tool called e-Project to close the interaction and communication gaps and enhance the overall learning process. As a result, online collaboration has become a backbone of the program's success. Through the use of e-Project's feature set—upgrade options from the basic collaborative product—EMBA students are able to transmit version-controlled documents with other study team members, pick up reading assignments and drop off homework, conduct online polls, and participate in discussion groups. Since the introduction of e-Project in 2001, Burke has also noticed a changing trend in how the software package is used by students, evolving from the practical to a pipeline to their peers and their relative areas of expertise.

Tech Talk ▼

By 2004, nearly 3 out of 4 youths will be using some form of wireless technology.
— Cahners Research, In-Stat Group ▲

"Last year we noticed that e-Project discussions tended to focus around ideas related to the program; homework questions and test complaints were typical," explains Burke. "As their experience with e-Project progressed, they began to see it as a collaborative tool to enhance business performance. One student was dealing with an ethical situation at work and decided to use e-Project to ask the other EMBA students for help and feedback on what to do."[12]

WIRELESS WONDERS AWAIT

For many companies, business is carried out through personal computers sitting on desktops, or laptops connected to networks via modems and phone lines. IBM engineers observed that operating business by "umbilical cords" can be cumbersome and restrictive.[13] Turning to wireless technology or m-commerce (mobile commerce) will help sever these ties. Mobile commerce refers to the conduct of e-commerce via wireless devices. According to International Data Corporation (IDC), by the end of 2002 the majority of Internet access will be through wireless rather than wired devices.[14]

As the workforce becomes increasingly decentralized through telecommuting and virtual teams, information and data become increasingly centralized, allowing for direct access by employees anywhere, anytime. So what are the implications for internal management communication under this model? IDC makes three predictions:

- "Corporate business travelers can access their company's internal networks while away from the office, perhaps from a client's office, an airport, hotel, or coffee shop. Many of them will make use of time that was otherwise 'wasted' waiting for appointments to begin."

- "When unexpected events occur, remote employees can be contacted immediately and proactively respond to minimize the negative business impact."
- "Telecommuters will be able to review their daily schedules and update them throughout the day. Increasingly, they will be able to access and download data and documents into handheld devices as well as access e-mail and conduct web searches with greater reliability and ease."[15]

According to the In-Stat Group of *Cahners' Wireless Week,* "m-commerce is currently one of the most heavily hyped sectors in high tech, but the hoopla may be out of proportion with reality." They point out that wireless devices are not user-friendly for data functions, especially those relying on rich graphics or high levels of data entry. They also express concerns about inadequate security to protect financial and other sensitive information transmitted via wireless devices.[16] Figure 2-1 illustrates predicted trends in m-commerce.

Despite high costs, steep learning curves, and security concerns, Notre Dame's Bill Brewster predicts that technically enhanced communication is here to stay and is limited in its prevalence and popularity mostly by issues concerning bandwidth rather than buy-in. He says that

Figure 2-1   Total Worldwide M-Commerce Users

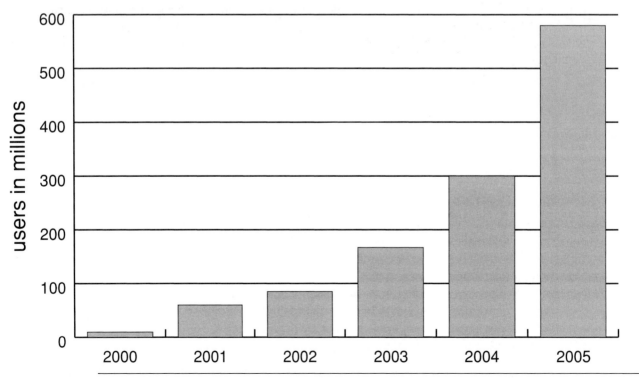

Source: Cahners' In-Stat Group. "Is M-Commerce Hype Unrealistic?" Retrieved July 10, 2001, from *http://www.instat.com/rh/wirelessweek/wp0101md.htm?sourceid=00383325532748954151*. Used by permission.

particularly since the September 11, 2001, attacks on the World Trade Center and the Pentagon, executives are increasingly interested in a videoconferencing alternative to business travel.

"We were inundated with calls from companies wanting to rent our equipment after September 11th," says Brewster. "Increasingly, managers want the ability to participate in meetings around the world without having to get on an airplane."[17]

WHAT DOES E-TECHNOLOGY MEAN FOR YOU AND YOUR BUSINESS?

The arrival of so much electronic technology so quickly will mean several things, for sure: First, you will have the opportunity to build teams across town and in time zones around the world, seeking business opportunities that would have been unthinkable just a decade ago. Second, it means that your employees, no matter where they live or happen to be working for the day, will have access to the same real-time information and processing capabilities as every other person in the company. That means instantaneous price quotes, up-to-the-moment stock inventories, and expert advice available to anyone at any hour of the day. It means fewer lost opportunities, closer relationships with clients, shorter product cycles, and dramatically decreased time-to-market spans.

Is all of this good? Well, much of it is, but it comes at a price. First, your firm will have to invest literally millions in new equipment, software applications, and training. And, just as you integrate the very latest in upgrades to your systems, something newer, cooler, and more expensive will come along. Senior management will be forced to continuously evaluate the equipment and systems they've invested in and decide—often on very short notice—when to replace them, keep them, fix them, or abandon them. Recycling processors, servers, hubs, and routers will be as commonplace as recycling aluminum cans in another ten years.

Problems other than investment will inevitably arise. There will be resisters, of course, who must be exhorted and encouraged to adopt new technologies. And many of them will have their worst fears confirmed when dazzling new software packages and can't-fail new devices fail unexpectedly or are . . . well, less than dazzling.

Beyond that, many of your best employees, colleagues, and friends will feel as though the distinction between office and home—between their professional and personal lives—has either blurred or disappeared altogether. If we're not careful about how we introduce and apply new technologies, our employees may come to resent both them and us. The temptation to tell them to use such new devices, opportunities, and applications is certainly great—we've paid a great deal of money for them and we're genuinely afraid the competition is up at night, using their new equipment. If we don't push our employees, we fear being left out, left behind, or crushed in the scramble to improve our business processes.

Let's keep in mind that while technology can offer us great leverage—the ability to lift and move with great strength—we must acknowledge that it's still our employees who are doing the lifting. Technology must offer them a way to improve their lives, not merely improve the firm's cash flow or profit margins. To be truly valuable, technology must offer us ways to improve the human condition and the quality of our lives. It can, of course, if we design, select, and use it properly. How we use technology each day in the workplace is the subject of the next chapter.

DISCUSSION QUESTIONS

1. How can managers use communication to help ease new users' fears of electronic technology?

2. What are the facilitator's role and objectives in the electronic technology training process?

3. Why is there not a one-size-fits-all solution when it comes to electronic technology?

4. Describe some of the key benefits of teleconferencing.

5. What are some of the collaboration tools or by-products generated through the engagement of collaboration applications?

ENDNOTES

1. J. Moxley. "Getting Past the Gatekeepers: Managing the Transition to Online Learning." Training Directors' Forum, June 10–13, 2001, Las Vegas, Nevada.
2. B. Brewster, Director of Technology, University of Notre Dame [interview].
3. M. Yurasek-Sexton. "Project Management, Web Projects and Collaboration." College of Business, University of Notre Dame, 2001.
4. B. Bruck. "How Companies Work: Creating Distributed Teams Online." A Caucus Consortium Whitepaper. Retrieved June 20, 2001, from *http://www.caucus.com/pdf/howcompanieswork.pdf.*
5. Ibid.
6. C. Soldatos, Marketing Communications Manager for the Business, Corporate, & Government Division of AAPT. Retrieved July 10, 2001, from *http://www.aapt.com.au/corpgov/teleconf/index.asp.* Used by permission.
7. T. Fairhead and R. Lewis. "A Field Study Examining Project Management and Collaborative Software in the Workforce." College of Business, University of Notre Dame, 1999.
8. Ian Lamont, Network World, 11/13/00. Retrieved July 8, 2001, from *http://www.virtualteams.com/company/press/itworld_lamont.htm.*
9. E. Vogt. "Professional Learning Communities: The Key to Success in the New Economy." Training Directors' Forum, June 10–13, 2001, Las Vegas, Nevada.
10. Brewster, personal interview.
11. L. Burke, Associate Dean and Director of Executive Education, University of Notre Dame [personal interview].
12. Ibid.
13 "A Wireless World Awaits: Nine Moves That Mobilize E-Business." Retrieved June 20, 2001, from *http://www-3.ibm.com/e-business/resource/pdf/44040.pdf.*
14. "IDC Envisions a Time When Majority of Internet Access Will Be Through Wireless Devices," IDC Corporate Press Release. Retrieved April 26, 2001, from *http://www.idc.com/communications/press/pr/cm041000pr.stm.*
15. Ibid.
16. Cahners' In-Stat Group. "Is M-Commerce Hype Unrealistic?" Retrieved June 21, 2001, from *http://www.instat.com/rh/wirelessweek/wp0101md.htm?sourceid=00383325532748954151.*
17. Brewster, personal inteview.

3 ONLINE WORKPLACE BEHAVIORS AND THE POLICIES THAT GUIDE THEM

Eric Rolfe Greenberg, director of management studies at the American Management Association (AMA) in New York, estimates that 45 percent of large U.S. companies monitor electronic mail (e-mail) communications, while more than three-quarters monitor some aspect of employee use of technology.[1] According to The Privacy Foundation, nearly 14 million U.S. workers may be under surveillance while using e-mail or surfing the 'Net, at an annual cost of about $10 per head.[2] So prevalent is the trend toward monitoring some aspect of employee use of communication technology that it is becoming increasingly rare to find companies without usage policies and the monitoring software to enforce them.

For the most part, e-mail administrators are concerned with e-mail that is oversized, that may slow other applications and tasks, or with messages containing worms and viruses that might infiltrate the intranet and cause extensive, costly damage. Indeed, some organizations reluctantly monitor e-mail just to ensure that their systems are not being bogged down by large inboxes.[3] Hacking and security leaks are other target problems, as are concerns for productivity and the fear of unethical, proprietary, or illegal content being sent or received by employees.

Some analysts say that the real point of monitoring e-mail is to provide a deterrent rather than punishment, which can mean costly prosecutions and dismissals. Yet dismissals for violations of e-mail policies are more frequent than ever—even *The New York Times* fired 23 employees for inappropriate use of e-mail during work time in 2001. The *Times* had allowed "reasonable" use of e-mail but found that the fired employees had breached standards of ethical and proper conduct. The news organization also indicated that it was deeply concerned about its liability in harassment suits if e-mail material that employees sent to one another were deemed offensive.[4]

Tech Talk ▼

Employee abuse of corporate-owned e-mail and Internet costs U.S. companies $54 billion each year.
— According to Websense, Inc.,
a San Diego-based software
development firm ▲

Whatever the reason, e-mail monitoring by employers has tripled in the past five years. What's more, corporate monitoring does not begin and end with e-mail. Employers also monitor web surfing activity, with a particular focus on sites that clearly are not related to company job descriptions. Visits to sites featuring online gambling, pornography, job search sites like http://www.Monster.com, and sports and gaming sites all raise the eyebrows of information technology administrators and fall well outside the limits of most web usage policies.

Disgruntled employees may argue that the personal use of e-mail at work has not diminished productivity in the least. They argue, in fact, that sending personal e-mail from work is justified, given the amount of time they devote to work while at home. They also argue that as long as the work gets done to the standards expected, then no harm comes from occasionally allowing private time to overlap with work time.

MONITORING: A BREACH OF PRIVACY OR A COMPANY'S RIGHT?

This chapter will discuss how communication managers can strike a balance between monitoring employee use of e-mail and the Internet versus concerns for employee privacy. We offer guidelines for how to manage an ever-increasing volume of e-mail, as well as suggestions for how employee policies can be written to protect the interests of the company regarding e-mail and web usage. Finally, we'll review e-mail writing guidelines for managers and employees alike.

Managers need to know with some measure of certainty what is passing through their technology systems, particularly if the content could be considered discriminatory, harassing, or pornographic. Because companies are liable for the use of this corporate asset, it is in their best interest to manage technology's use. Special monitoring software that manages that task electronically has taken much of the work out of this practice, along with lowering the overall cost. As you'll see in Table 3-1, more than three-quarters of U.S. companies monitor some aspect of their employees' use of technology—from e-mail to web use to voice mail. They are twice as likely to do so as five years ago, and most now use monitoring software to manage the task.

Table 3-1   Percentage of Companies That Monitor Employees

Level of Monitoring*	1997	2001
Total active monitoring	35.3%	77.1%
Monitoring Internet connections	54.1%	62.8%
Storage and review of e-mail messages	14.9%	46.5%
Storage and review of computer files	13.7%	36.1%
Recording/reviewing phone conversations	10.4%	11.9%
Storage and review of voice-mail messages	5.3%	7.8%

*Excluding telephone logs, logging on/off computer, and normal video surveillance for security purposes.

Source: Adapted from *U.S. News and World Report,* April 30, 2001.

Another major justification for monitoring of this nature is loss of employee productivity because of time spent online. International Data Corporation reports that approximately 30 to 40 percent of lost productivity is due directly to employees using work time to surf the 'Net. On pornographic web sites, up to 70 percent of traffic takes place during work hours.[5] Internally circulated e-mails have also become an issue with some companies such as Chevron and Microsoft, with both settling millions of dollars worth of sexual harassment lawsuits.[6]

Clearly, the case for monitoring electronic communications is strong on its own merits. Communication managers needn't look far if they want further convincing of the increasingly prevalent practice. But if they need an additional nudge, numerous application providers of monitoring software use web site promotions to first promote the need for their product and then allow it to be downloaded (see Figure 3-1). From http://www.surfcontrol.com come the following questions and issues for managers on the monitor-or-not-to-monitor fence:

Figure 3-1   Web Usage by Category

SurfControl categorizes web usage by site type and graphically displays where employees spend the most time online.

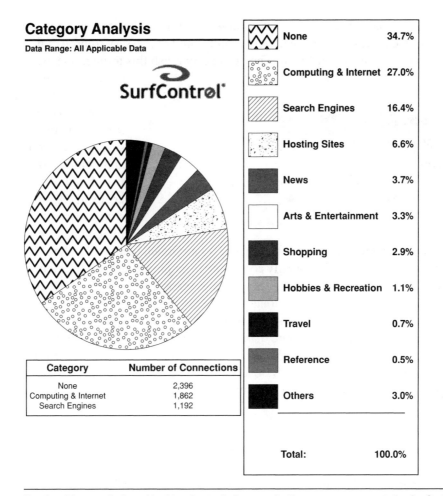

Reprinted by permission of Ignition Strategic Communications, press representative for SurfControl.

- **"Enhancing employee productivity.** From last night's sports scores to online games and day trading, the Internet is a seductive place. How many hours of lost productivity can your company afford?
- **Optimizing network bandwidth.** Combine recreational surfing with bandwidth-intensive activities such as streaming audio and video and MP3 downloads and you have a significant effect on network performance.
- **Reducing legal liability.** Letting employees surf anywhere on the Internet can permit them to stray to clearly inappropriate sites: sexually explicit sites and those promoting violence and hate speech. This can lead, in turn, to lawsuits, harassment charges, and even criminal prosecution. Protect your employees and your company by promoting intelligent Internet use.
- **Analyzing web site categories.** Analyzing which category of web site each employee is accessing can be helpful. Employers can then ensure employees are accessing sites that are relevant to their job descriptions."[7]

POLICIES THAT PROTECT AND SERVE

To come to terms with the issue of whether to monitor employees, managers must communicate with and educate employees about why monitoring is necessary to protect the company and its assets—both human and financial. They can accomplish this through the use of comprehensive e-mail and web usage policies, which may be similar in structure to employee policies governing the use of other corporate assets such as telephones, fax machines, and copiers. By 2001, more than two-thirds of the American Management Association's membership had written policies in place for company e-mail, and 11 percent said they were drafting policies at the time. Organizations like the AMA recognize that having clear guidelines will not only contribute to employee support for monitoring but will also help with any potential litigation issues. If your company doesn't have such a policy in place, it's clearly out of step with the national trend.

Tech Talk ▼

Nearly 63 percent of companies monitor employee voice mail messages.
— According to a 2000 study by the American Management Association ▲

Policies run the gamut from single statements disallowing any use of technology for nonwork reasons to documents of more than 20 pages in length that all employees must periodically review and sign. Commonly reviewed during new-hire orientation, these policies often appear on corporate intranets as reminders of acceptable use.

Regardless of length, the best of e-mail and web policy documents often share a number of ingredients in common:

- **Legal.** The document should clearly state that noncompliance by users may result in denial or removal of access privileges, disciplinary action, civil litigation, or criminal prosecution.
- **Productivity.** The policy should set forth guidelines for appropriate use, emphasizing that the resources exist in order to advance the company's goals and mission.

- **Definition of user.** Any person operating equipment that is owned by the company or that is available through a corporate facility. This equipment includes computer, networking, and telephone resources. Users may include consultants hired by the company, as well as part- and full-time employees.
- **Definition of policy violations.** The document should describe specific actions that are considered violations. These violations often include sending bulk messages; harassing or malicious messages; messages revealing proprietary, restricted, or confidential corporate data; or messages sent under another person's identity. Additionally, many policies set limits on the appropriate use of e-mail—for example, a maximum message size of 4MB; a message lifetime, with unchecked messages being deleted after 45 days; and a maximum number of messages, with a limit of 200 per mailbox. Finally, most policies forbid the use of encryption or the process of scrambling access codes to different computer programs to prevent detection of inappropriate use of communication technology.
- **Accountability.** Policies usually assign responsibility to an individual or department for ensuring compliance. This responsibility often falls under the direction of an information services and technology department.[8]

Aside from sections addressing each of these issues, most e-mail and web policies also rest on five major provisions:

1. The company owns the technology that supports e-mail and web usage, so it has the right to monitor usage. This includes the content contained within e-mail messages.
2. Technology exists to support activities consistent with corporate goals; other uses are subject to regulation.
3. At peak use, department heads must allocate technology resources according to priority.
4. The company will control or refuse access by violators of these procedures.
5. Any expectation of privacy by employees is balanced against a reasonable right of employers to supervise.

E-MAIL AND WEB POLICY DEVELOPMENT

While popular web sites such as http://www.email-policy.com offer one-size-fits-all policies that are more than adequate for some companies, many others will require a customized approach to policy development. These organizations often are attempting to juggle issues of employee productivity versus privacy by finding a healthy balance between protecting corporate assets and allowing for individual discretion with personal use of technology.

A customized approach to e-mail and web policy development typically begins with a brainstorming session, gathering a diverse group of employees to serve as a policy-drafting committee to discuss concerns, goals, and expectations for the policy. This group often comprises information technology experts, legal counsel, the company's ethics manager, a human resources representative, and members of key departments. The committee's function is to create an acceptable usage policy embodying the company's mission and how information technology helps to further it. One option is to follow this policy with a list of appropriate uses. The acceptable use policy frequently distinguishes between what is considered personal and what is regarded as professional use, with specific guidelines for appropriate personal use.

Suggestions for inappropriate personal use might include anything that interferes with employee responsibilities or is not in accordance with the corporation's mission, or which may result in inefficient operation of IT resources or anything prohibited by law. Commercialization clauses are also helpful to avoid exploitation of corporate resources for personal gain. After specifying acceptable use comes the delicate matter of unacceptable use. The unacceptable use policy should reflect the issues outlined in the employee handbook under the areas of discrimination, sexual harassment, and unprofessional conduct. This, too, can be followed with a list of unacceptable uses of other corporate technology.

Anything not specifically included in the acceptable and unacceptable use policies should be incorporated into a general disclaimer. The disclaimer should absolve the company of responsibility for damages to individual users when they access outside resources such as web sites and chat rooms. The disclaimer should always be as broad and general as possible, to offer the greatest measure of protection for the company. It should also remind users the e-mail that has been sent and deleted remains stored on backup systems for some time.

After the policy is outlined, key technology terms should be listed with definitions. The most important terms are administrator, commercial use, information technology resources (individual, networked, and shared), unofficial web sites, and user. The company should also appoint a committee to review the policy annually and make adjustments in response to changes in the law and information technology.

RESPONSIBILITY OF USERS

Users of corporate communication technologies have a number of responsibilities. At most companies with such policies, all employees with access to e-mail and the web must read, sign, date, and return a Use Agreement before they are granted access privileges. These documents should clearly and concisely outline the responsible use of electronic resources. This definition often covers several areas:

- **Professional considerations.** Respect the rights of others, protect confidentiality, and protect system security.
- **Technology-specific requirements.** Don't share passwords, don't threaten or harass, don't hack into systems, and don't violate copyright protections or other laws.
- **E-mail-specific requirements.** Messages should be company-related and professional.
- **Explanation of policy violation consequences.** Polices range in severity from denial or removal of access privileges to disciplinary action, civil litigation, or criminal prosecution.[9]

POLICY IMPLEMENTATION

Employees need to understand e-mail and web policies in order to be held accountable for them. In addition to understanding their content, it's always helpful if employees understand what motivates this sort of concern by the company. At the very least, this will require training sessions to introduce and explain the company's e-mail policy and to highlight best practices for e-mail use. An informed employee who understands why he is being monitored is more likely to

Tech Talk ▼

An astonishing 37 percent of employees surveyed report constantly surfing the web at work for personal reasons.
— www.Vault.com, June 2000 ▲

exhibit the behavior management hopes to reinforce. And, as most experienced managers know, participation fosters acceptance.

Besides conducting a thorough overview on the policy, training sessions should also outline appropriate e-mail etiquette. Messages can cause significant harm to a company and its reputation, even when no laws have been violated. A number of cases have been documented in which the content of messages has been published or forwarded in a way that proves embarrassing to a company or its representatives.

ADDITIONAL GUIDELINES FOR E-MAIL EFFICIENCY

Once employees understand when (and how) they may and may *not* use e-mail, the next step is to make sure they use it efficiently and effectively. E-mail is one channel choice for communication that risks overuse because of its convenience and ease of operation. But its very lack of formality makes it inappropriate for some communication interactions, such as hiring or terminating employees, expressing condolences, or sending news to a friend or relative over the holidays. And never send office memos via e-mail to reprimand employees, as the personal nature of that communication is easily forwarded to others within the organization.[10]

Some common do's and don'ts for managing and sending e-mails from the workplace include the following suggestions.

Tech Talk ▼

"The Great Promise of Cyberspace is speed. Along with the grinding efficiency of it all, just a few thoughtful words can change the entire nature of communication. Good manners mean a quiet touch of warmth in the cold new techno world."
— Letitia Baldrige, author of *The New Complete Guide to Executive Manners* ▲

Do:

- Attend training sessions (if they exist) to fully understand the proper application of the e-mail policy and to highlight best practices for e-mail use.
- Keep your e-mail policy concise—no more than 15 pages. Make sure the document describes those specific actions that are considered policy violations, including sending bulk messages, harassing or malicious messages, or messages under another person's identity.
- Be careful with your e-mail grammar, spelling, sentence structure, and punctuation. Errors of this sort can damage your credibility just as easily online as on paper.
- Use a greeting, closing, and purpose statement for each e-mail message, and make a personal reference, if possible.

- Check carefully before clicking the Send button to avoid inadvertently sending e-mail to inappropriate recipients.
- Make sure the e-mail you send complies with the company's policies and is not offensive to other members of the organization.

DON'T:

- Ever send angry, demanding e-mail messages.
- Use e-mail bulletin boards as gossip corners, particularly where the gossip degenerates into defamation, harassment, and unprofessional conduct.
- Allow your saved and sent files to build up over time and bog down other network tasks.[11]

DISCUSSION QUESTIONS

1. Why do an increasing number of companies monitor how their employees use electronic technology such as e-mail and the Internet?

2. Exactly what do managers look for when they monitor employee use of electronic technology?

4. How prevalent are written corporate policies outlining expectations for employee use of electronic technology, and what do they look like?

4. What are some common provisions covered in the majority of formal corporate e-mail policies?

5. How can managers involve their employees in the process of creating an e-mail policy acceptable to all?

ENDNOTES

1. T. York. "Invasion of Privacy? E-mail Monitoring Is on the Rise." Retrieved June 26, 2001, from *http://www.informationweek.com/774/email.htm.*
2. B. Sullivan. "Study: One-Third of Workers Watched." MSNBC News, July 7, 2001.
3. L. Guernsey. "You've Got Inappropriate Mail," *The New York Times,* April 5, 2000, pp. C1, C10.
4. A. Carns. "Those Bawdy E-Mails Were Good for a Laugh—Until the Axe Fell," *Wall Street Journal,* February 4, 2000, pp. A1, A8.
5. "Workers, Surf at Your Own Risk." *Business Week,* June 12, 2000, p. 105.
6. Ibid.
7. Retrieved August 10, 2001, from *http://www.surfcontrol.com/products/superscout_for_business/ super_scout/.* Reprinted by permission of Ignition Strategic Communications, press representative for SurfControl.
8. University of Notre Dame MBA research assistants Matthew Boulger and Joseph Kosek are acknowledged for their research on e-mail policies and their effective implementation in the workplace.
9. Ibid.
10. Guernsey, op.cit. *The New York Times,* April 5, 2001, p. C-1.
11. R. Strauss. "You've Got Maelstrom," *The New York Times,* July 5, 2001, p. D-1.

4 E-LEARNING AS A COMMUNICATION AND COLLABORATION TOOL

One of the critical components changing the way management communication occurs in the workplace is e-learning. Employees must continuously synthesize new knowledge (through information, training, and industry observation) and build strategies that will ensure competitiveness in the knowledge economy. This is the essence of work today. What, then, is the role of management in the fourth economy if employees are able to manage their own work and use their colleagues' knowledge-sharing to sound out new ideas? Will this fundamentally change the way we work and, in turn, change the way we communicate within and between organizations? If the evolution of human learning theory is any guide, the answer is unquestionably "yes."

WHAT IS E-LEARNING?

How corporations communicate with and train their employees is just one example of how the Internet has fundamentally changed the way we learn. Estimates are that the corporate market for e-learning will be more than $11 billion by 2003. It was $2.2 billion in 2000.[2]

So how is e-learning defined? According to C. J. DeSantis, president of eLearners.com Inc., whether online, web-based, or technology-enhanced, e-learning is any form of learning that uses "a

Tech Talk ▼

"Certainly the 'Net is a powerful medium for communication. But even more important, it is a vocational medium—a place where real work gets done, real competitive advantage is gained, and real growth is generated."

— Lou Gerstner, IBM Chairman and Chief Executive Officer ▲

network for delivery, interaction, or facilitation (in a few years you might not even use a computer). The network could be the Internet, a school or college LAN [local area network] or even a corporate WAN [wide area network]. The learning could take place individually (guided or instructed by a computer) or as part of a class. Online classes could meet either synchronously (at the same time) or asynchronously (at different times), or in some combination of the two."[3]

According to educational expert Jay Cross, e-learning is a vision of what corporate training can become. Its hallmarks are

- "Learning on Internet-age steroids: often real-time, 24/7, anywhere, anytime.
- Learner-centered, personalized to the individual and customized to the organization.
- Network-assisted, often assembling learning experiences on the fly.
- A blend of learning methods: classroom, simulation, collaboration, community, and the traditional classroom.
- The entire range of learning phases, from assessment through testing and sometimes certification.
- Online administration: handling registration, payment and charge-backs, and monitoring learner progress."[4]

In addition, e-learning consultant Dorman Woodall says e-learning is sometimes referred to as "enterprise learning because the entire organization profits from it." He goes on to cite other definitions for the e, including that of "electronic learning because of its convenient method of delivery," "everywhere learning because it reaches more people in more locations than has ever been possible before," and "excellent learning because it is designed to accommodate the individual learner."[5]

CHARACTERISTICS OF E-LEARNING

Several characteristics define e-learning. First of all, e-learning is dynamic. Training and related expertise about any subject must be current and relevant, not old news or shelfware. This means that e-learning must provide online experts, the best sources, and fast solutions.

According to Woodall, "the context of e-learning is to operate in real time, making the best use of the technology, since both the content and the expert advice has to be there when you need it. Collaboration is used to leverage the explicit and tacit knowledge of the colleagues, experts, and professional peers. Thus, the job of e-learning is to bring resources together, from both inside and outside [the] organization,"[6] making each employee's job not only easier but also possible in the first place.

WHO ARE THE SUCCESSFUL E-LEARNERS?

What makes a successful online student? According to Jay Cross of Internet Time Group, the following characteristics are common to those who gain the most from the e-learning experience. Unlike learners in a traditional classroom situation (see Figure 4-1), these individuals tend to be

- Open-minded about sharing life, work, and educational experiences as part of the learning process;
- Able to communicate through writing;
- Self-motivated and self-disciplined;
- Accepting of critical thinking and decision making as part of the learning process; and
- Able to think ideas through before responding.[7]

Figure 4-1   A Traditional Instructor-Centric Paradigm

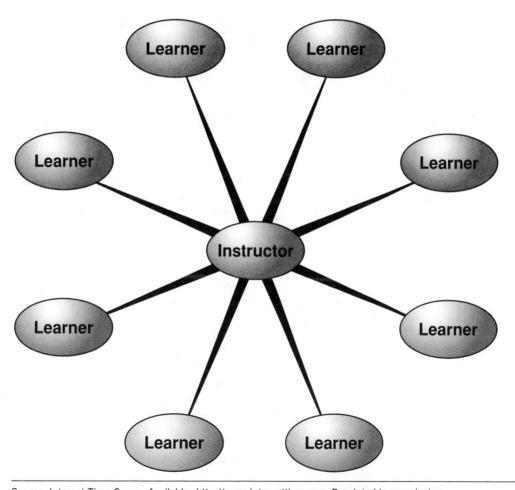

Source: Internet Time Group. Available: *http://www.internettime.com*. Reprinted by permission.

According to the Illinois Online Network, students who usually sit in the back of the class-room and avoid speaking in class frequently blossom in the online environment. Those students are more willing to risk written participation than spoken, perhaps partly because they can rethink and edit e-mail before sending it. And in the online environment, the visual barriers that prevent some people from expressing themselves are largely eliminated (see Figure 4-2).

Figure 4-2   A Networked Learner-Centric Paradigm

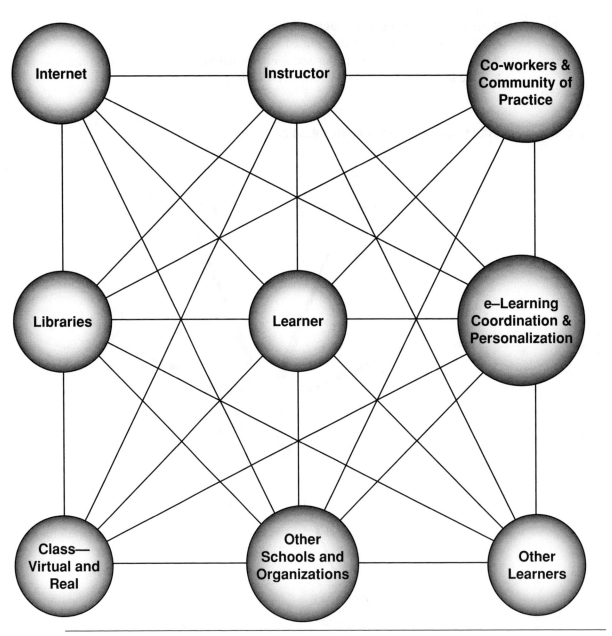

Source: J. Cross, "Leveraging the People Value Chain: E-Business Necessity," Internet Time Group. Retrieved September 17, 2000, from *http://www.internettime.com/itimegroup/peoplevaluechain.htm*. Reprinted by permission.

The circle of learners in a corporation can be expanded through e-learning, as can the number and frequency of learning occasions. Indeed, one of the primary advantages of e-learning comes from increasing the top line—"enabling organizations to do things they couldn't do with traditional training. Examples of these enhancements include transforming a traditional business into an e-business and certifying thousands of employees in technical disciplines, to name just two."[8]

What's more, there is value created for an organization when its employees are not tied up in training during normal business hours. "A corporate communication director's time during working hours is worth much more than the same individual's time after closing time or in a nonpeak season for the company. E-learning often enables an employee to shift learning to those nonpeak hours."[9]

Woodall states that "the power of e-learning via the Internet brings increased personalized services and an individualized approach to the learner." In true just-in-time fashion, each learner should be able to select from educational opportunities that pertain to his or her unique background, job, and career. Furthermore, Woodall notes that "e-learning provides learning events from many sources enabling the learner to select a favorite format or learning method," whether synchronous, asynchronous, or a combination of both. "The full context of e-learning means the learner is allowed to actively construct his or her own learning experience without having to rely on direction from a teacher."[10]

A list of words in Table 4-1 compares learning in the Industrial Age versus learning in the fourth economy. The lesson here is clear: E-learning is clearly more fun.

Tech Talk ▼

Estimates are that the corporate market for e-learning will be over $11 billion by 2003. It was $2.2 billion in 2000.
— *The New York Times*, April 18, 2001 ▲

Table 4-1   Learning in the Industrial Age versus Learning in the Fourth Economy

Industrial Age	Fourth Economy
Training	Learning
Passive	Interactive
Listen	Learn by doing
Alone	Community
Teaching	Apprenticeship
Just-in-case	Just-in-time
Classroom	Anywhere
Absorb	Experiment
Graduate	In perpetuity

Source: J. Cross, Internet Time Group. Retrieved July 5, 2001, from *http://www.internetttime.com/itimegroup/elearning/networks.htm*. Reprinted by permission.

Clearly, successful e-learning must be simulation-based and highly interactive, an approach that blends many different learning tools. For example, knowledge management and e-learning converge into content management as more knowledge content is being developed and placed into online libraries where knowledge can easily be shared. Very often, projects are innovative and often contain reusable content, once again encouraging knowledge sharing within an organization.

TYPES OF E-LEARNING

U.S.-based organizations spend by far the greatest amount of their training dollars on computer applications. Close to 80 percent of all employees received training in this area or on other topics with software applications in 2000.[11] Almost 40 percent of all employer-sponsored training in the United States is designed and implemented to teach computer skills. This training, of course, includes everything from an introductory course in Microsoft Office to advanced training in programming or systems engineering.

Computer-delivered training occurs from CD-ROM (40 percent), online via an internal computer network (31 percent), online via the Internet (19 percent), from floppy disk (7 percent), or via the computer by other means (4 percent). Some 71 percent of online learning occurs solely between the trainee and the computer, while 29 percent of online interaction occurs with a human instructor and other students.

In the majority of cases (58 percent), information technology (IT) training is designed offshore or by non-U.S. organizations. Internal departments deliver IT training more than half the time, with 45 percent of delivery being outsourced.[12]

FACTORS INFLUENCING E-LEARNING

For most companies, success is best achieved through "a blended approach to learning within the organization. This includes classroom instruction, team meetings, demonstrations, exercises, newsletters, e-mail, self-paced courseware, resource centers, virtual classes, live chats, asynchronous discussions, mentoring, and simulations."[13] Simulation software lets novices and employees at the intermediate level tap into expert knowledge from those who have many more years of experience. Blending the classroom with web-based training is working well for many companies, including "Circuit City for sales force training, American Airlines for flight attendant training; and MasterCard International, which now offers a course on dealing with sexual harassment."[14]

Implementing e-learning that is as effective as possible in your company requires a shift in the management paradigm regarding how knowledge strategy is perceived. The old paradigm dictated that individuals must contribute to or access information from a variety of sources—the individual is the center of the knowledge-management paradigm.

The new paradigm for knowledge management requires that individuals contribute to or access information from a single, virtual resource. A new knowledge strategy supports communication and collaboration through these virtual communities. Other benefits to adopting the new paradigm include

- "Practice in a low-risk environment;
- Increased complexity in scoring and feedback;
- A higher level of learner engagement—the program is self-paced;
- Teaching self-evaluation; and
- Expert decisions retained within the company, even when the employee leaves."[15]

DEALING WITH DROPOUTS

Just as in traditional learning environments, some students will embrace the e-learning educational experience more enthusiastically than others. Fear of technology is a common excuse for dropouts, as is the rationale that the old way is somehow preferable to the new, electronic approach. Executive MBA Program technology director Bill Brewster frequently deals with techno-phobic managers but has also seen firsthand how intuitive training and support can help boost adaptation rates of new technology.

> **Tech Talk ▼**
>
> *"Learning technologies encompass the processes through which tools, technologies, people, and information join together to impart knowledge to a particular audience."*[16]
>
> — John Redmon, "Successful Strategies for WBT Development" ▲

"Three years ago the comfort level with our distance learning technology was very low, both for students and faculty," explains Brewster. "It took a lot of prodding to get our remote students involved. But we've seen a dramatic increase with the acceptance of the technology, as people have seen firsthand how it works and that it works."[17]

Managers such as Brewster can do several things to keep dropouts to a minimum and to motivate discouraged learners to return to the flock. According to Eric Parkes, Ph.D., President and CEO of ASK International, there are several ways to help keep e-learners on track:

- "Use the three-click rule (no single task should require more than three clicks, helping the user to feel less lost in the technology).
- Label the site with compatible browsers and recommend access speed. If certain software requires a T-1 line to work effectively, do not say that a 28.8K modem is acceptable.
- Warn of the need to use plug-ins, particularly if the remote user gets booted off the system routinely. How do they quickly get back into training?
- Provide the human element for contact so that the remote user can ask questions.
- Don't expect the remote user to read scroll text or pages of noninteractive material. Provide an interesting learning experience. Make sure the site has attractive, engaging content.
- Ensure access, both physically and also when on site. A clear site map is imperative in helping remote users get where they want to be.
- Articulate e-learning values; ensure that they nourish the remote user's human spirit and address what's really in it for them—helping to create a true learning community."[18]

ARE YOUR EMPLOYEES READY FOR E-LEARNING?

One certain way to alienate your employees, waste valuable time and training dollars, and lower productivity in your organization is to purchase or implement an e-learning system or program before your employees are ready. The obvious question, then, is "How do you know when they're ready?" Have a look at the questionnaires contained in Appendix A, The E-Learning Readiness Scale. The simple, easy-to-administer instruments will tell you

- Whether your employees are ready to begin training with the use of e-technology,
- How to design questions about e-learning instructional processes,
- How to assess instructional content questions,
- How to assess e-learning features questions,
- How to assess the effectiveness of mentoring services,
- How to assess supplier support,
- How to assess e-learning deployment systems, and
- How to assess supplier credentials.

The e-learning readiness questionnaire features a ten-point rating scale and a simple method of determining whether your employees are ready for a step of this sort. The other questionnaires in the Appendix are based on yes or no replies or open-ended responses. In each case, the manager responsible for e-learning investment and achievement of training goals must decide whether the appropriate balance of positive replies is present. The questionnaires won't guarantee success, of course, but, at the very least, they will give managers accountable for such programs a range of issues to consider and some sense of what successful programs look like.

WHAT DOES E-LEARNING MEAN TO YOU?

All of this certainly looks interesting and, to some, looks exciting. But what does it mean for you and the organizations that you'll work for in the years ahead? For one thing, it means that your education cannot stop with graduation from a degree program in residence. When you pack up your books, CDs, and memories of college and put the ivy-covered walls in the rearview mirror, you must recognize that your education has only begun (remember, that's why they call it commencement). Your employers will provide you with training, of course, in a variety of venues across a full range of topics. But your education (values-based instruction that differs from task-oriented training) can and must continue.

"I'll have an MBA by then," you say. "How much education do I need?" The answer to that question has almost nothing to do with additional degrees and almost everything to do with how current your education is. How soon will you need to update the learning you acquired in school? What new subjects will you have to take on when you change jobs? As technology, society, and the workplace change, will you be ready? You will if you allow e-learning to become a regular part of your life. E-learning will offer you access to topics, instructors, ideas, images, and experiences that your parents never dreamed of. The real advantage of the fourth economy, after all, is the opportunity to share ideas without having to give them away.

And, if it works for you, why wouldn't it work for your employees? We hear regular complaints about the elementary and secondary school systems in this country but few suggestions for reform that involve the workplace. Investing in your workforce, providing them with skills, opportunity, and motivation, is certainly one way to ensure that your firm isn't left behind as the fourth economy becomes increasingly dependent on ideas and mind work. If the learning programs available on disk or online are unappealing to you, ask why. What can the vendor do to improve the quality, interest level, or relevance of the programs and their content? A huge number of competitors are now actively involved in a $10-billion- plus market. More than just a few of them are interested in your business.

Finally, Jeff Bernel, Chairman and former CEO of American Rubber Products Company, may have figured out what the real value of continuous e-learning is. "I could literally take what I had downloaded onto my laptop from my Executive MBA course one evening and put it to work in my business the next day. I mean it," he said. "I paid for the cost of that instruction ten times over before I was ever done with the program."[19]

DISCUSSION QUESTIONS

1. How is e-learning defined?

2. What are the characteristics of a successful online student?

3. What are some words you could use to describe the Industrial Age? What are some words you could use to describe the fourth economy?

4. How do many companies define success as applied to e-learning, and how does the role of participants contribute to that success?

5. How can managers increase the likelihood that an inhouse e-learning program will be successful?

ENDNOTES

1. E. R. Parkes. "Why Online Learners Drop Out and What to Do About It." Training Directors' Forum, June 10–13, 2001, Las Vegas, Nevada. Retrieved July 18, 2001, from *http://www.askintl.com.*

2. S. Stellan. *The New York Times,* April 18, 2001.

3. C. J. DeSantis. eLearners.com Inc. Retrieved July 16, 2001, from *http://elearners.com/ elearning/q1.asp.*

4. J. Cross. Internet Time Group. Retrieved July 20, 2001, from *http://www.internettime.com/ itimegroup/more.htm.*

5. Permission granted by Dorman Woodall, e-Learning Consultant. Retrieved July 10, 2001, from *http://www.internettime.com/itimegroup/woodall.htm#_Toc484301695.*

6. Ibid.

7. J. Cross. Internet Time Group. Retrieved July 20, 2001, from *http://www.internettime.com/ itimegroup/people/learners.htm.*

8. S. Stellan. *The New York Times,* April 18, 2001.

9. J. Cross. Internet Time Group e-learning jump page. Retrieved July 25, 2001, from *http://www.internettime.com/itimegroup/metrics.htm.*

10. Woodall.

11. Industry Report 2000 *Training* magazine. Presented at 17th Annual Training Directors' Forum, June 10–13, 2001, Las Vegas, Nevada.

12. Ibid.

13. K. Fullerton. "E-Learning Communities: The Missing Link." Presentation at Training Directors' Forum, June 10–13, 2001, Las Vegas, Nevada.
14. S. Stellan. *The New York Times,* April 18, 2001.
15. B. Hughes and R. Park. "Creating Expertise through Cognitive Task Simulations." Training Directors' Forum, June 10–13, 2001, Las Vegas, Nevada.
16. Permission granted by John Redmon, The Redmon Group.
17. B. Brewster. Technology Director, Executive MBA Program, University of Notre Dame [interview]. Personal interview conducted February 15, 2002.
18. Parkes.
19. J. Bernel, personal communication, February 2002.

5 WHAT ARE VIRTUAL TEAMS?

The CEO lived in Columbus, the senior partner worked from Chicago, the director of sales was based in San Francisco, and a few others worked out of their basements. Very few of them were ever in the same ZIP Code, yet the Eagles.Net team was able to manage fundraising campaigns for more than 300 nonprofit groups over a five-year window, helping them collectively raise more than $50 million.

Companies like Eagles.Net are pioneering a new way to work. Increasingly, we communicate with our co-workers and teammates in new ways, relying on virtual teams to get things done. For many of these companies, gone are regular face-to-face interactions with colleagues who inhabit the same building. Instead, virtual teams have been formed—groups of people collaborating through technology to meet a client or organizational need.[1] Often, they are working from a home office. These workers are not co-located for a significant part of their working day but are responsible for the production of specific work products for which their collaboration is required to produce deliverables.[2]

Tech Talk ▼

"Today's worker can be reached by cell phone, pager, e-mail, and fax—but is often isolated from the rest of the office team and works with people from other organizations all the time."
— Jessica Lipnack, CEO,
VirtualTeams.com ▲

The growing number of home-based workers—nearly 24 million in 2000[3]—coupled with the move by organizations to expand globally, has compounded the number of permanent yet virtual teams. Indeed, virtual teams are fast becoming the rule rather than the exception in many organizations. That's because much of what once took place via face-to-face communication can be managed online. This includes

- Assigning tasks,
- Making decisions,
- Resolving conflicts,
- Providing leadership,

- Designating accountability, and
- Facilitating meetings.[4]

"Teamwork has been around since before our ancestors gathered up their spears and learned how to work together to gang up on mastodons and saber-toothed tigers," says David Gould, Campus Department Chair for Information Systems and Technology at the University of Phoenix. "Many experts agree that teams are the primary unit of performance in any organization. Today there is a new kind of team—a 'virtual' team made up of people who communicate electronically. Its members may hardly ever see each other in person. In fact, they may never meet at all, except in cyberspace."[5] Research has shown that while most virtual team members have positive experiences overall, the biggest area of complaint involves communication problems.[6] Two major issues are lack of project visibility, or seeing and understanding the big picture, and tracking down people to obtain timely responses for information. Dealing with those complaints requires planning the communication process of virtual teams from start to finish. Experts on virtual teaming suggest that you consider these specific actions:

- Assess each member of your target audience, including each one's level of technical competence.
- Develop a communication plan that will help support and accept initiatives and ensure data that can be used to prove effectiveness of the strategy.
- Recognize that team members are going to require access to information—and each other—from anytime, anywhere.
- Communicate continuously throughout the project (include interesting stories, features, and more).
- Develop formal and informal feedback loops.
- Employ good intranet communication among employees, managers, and others involved in virtual teams, both within and outside of the organization. The intranet should contain useful information for all stakeholders and be kept as up-to-date as possible.
- Create a culture of open access that encourages knowledge sharing and trust.
- Share your purposes and goals. Accountability involves all participants. Share responsibility for tracking, measurement, and follow-up tasks, and share credit for outcomes, as well.

The most important consideration when implementing virtual teams in the workplace is to remember that people are the key to success.[7] Whatever Internet tools are implemented, they must make work *easier* for the team involved. It is especially important that team members perceive their workload as being more manageable through the technologically advanced tools they are using. The major focus must be on people and how e-technology tools can help them become more efficient and effective. Gould suggests that other ways communication managers can help improve virtual team communication include

- Giving team members a sense of how the overall project is going;
- Not letting team members vanish from the communication loop for long periods of time;
- Establishing opportunities for face-to-face communication, if possible;
- Establishing a code of conduct to avoid delays in feedback; and
- Augmenting text-only communication with examples.[8]

BARRIERS TO VIRTUAL WORK

Data compiled by M.I.T. Professor Tom Allen over the past several decades shows how the probability of communicating diminishes as the distance in separation grows greater (see Figure 5-1). The closer the proximity, the greater the collaboration.[9] His findings have obvious implications for any team but are especially noteworthy for those working virtually.

Figure 5-1   The Relationship of Proximity to Frequency of Communication

How Close Is Close?

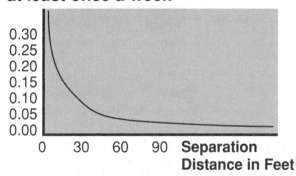

Office Location	Probability of Research Collaboration
Same Corridor	10.3%
Same floor	1.9%
Different floor	0.3%
Different buildings	0.4%

Based on proximity, people are not likely to collaborate very often if they are more than 50 feet apart.

Source: T. J. Allen, *Managing the Flow of Technology: Technology Transfer and the Dissemination of Technological Information within the R&D Organization* (Cambridge, Mass.: M.I.T. Press, 1977). Reprinted by permission.

Allen's findings offer several important implications for the communication protocols of virtual teams. These might include

- **"Time zone challenges.** Communications managers may find themselves spending as much energy planning the communication process as they do implementing it. That's because they must define the mix of face-to-face, virtual real-time (synchronous; i.e., telephone), and non-real-time exchanges (asynchronous; i.e., e-mail).
- **Seeing the work versus seeing each other.** Team members must be able to see what work needs to be done, all the time, regardless of where they are, and they must be absolutely sure they are looking at the latest version of something.
- **Building trust.** Face-to-face interaction is the fastest way to build trust, crucial in the early phases of virtual team life.
- **Clear project goals.** Virtual teams spend more time on task mechanics and on planning what they're going to do compared with traditional office-based workgroups. If project goals aren't clear from the beginning, chances for success are low.
- **Learning to be proactive.** Workers must be very proactive; they can't simply sit somewhere and wait for information to come to them. They need to be aggressive and communicate electronically with high levels of energy.
- **Learning to make decisions.** Decision-making changes in crisis situations for virtual team members. In an office environment, a manager will typically consult with a group of people before making decisions. Online, however, team members will typically select the best person to solve the dilemma."[10]

Tech Talk ▼

"While Valent Software's ten employees were never really co-located, they were able to sell their $700,000 investment and three years of work for $45 million to a major web portal."

— Jessica Lipnack, CEO,
VirtualTeams.com ▲

Barriers to connectivity are also found within virtual teams.[11] These obstacles seem to be primarily social and economic in nature. The challenge is getting individuals in different locations to function as a cohesive unit. And every culture—vocational culture, company culture, national culture—has its own set of principles, habits, and norms. Because virtual teams live on communication, a single set of assumptions about communication and what it means to say X and do Y is essential to ensure the success of virtual teams. Gould states that this would include

- **Language.** How can we talk to others around the globe?
- **Multicultural diversity.** How do we transcend our own cultural frame of reference?
- **Trust.** How can we build relationships as we enter into electronic dialogues?
- **Cognitive accessibility.** How can we increase the technical comfort level of those who don't (or won't) participate?
- **Affordability.** How can we make open communications and knowledge exchange profitable, yet affordable?[12]

SELECTING TEAM TOOLS

The tools or software you select for virtual team communication must fit snugly with your organization's objectives. There must be a good fit between what your organization and virtual team are trying to achieve and what the tool can actually do to increase progress toward that goal.[13] Currently there is no tool or software that can replace the human factor—and it is the human factor that is so critical for effective work success. And, central to that human factor is successful communication. Remember that, throughout all virtual team interactions, conversation must be at the core—not at the periphery.

Bill Bruck of Caucus Systems in Arlington, Virginia, has written extensively on what virtual teams must do to succeed. His firm, a leading provider of online collaborative environments for Global 1000 companies, offers this advice:

- **"Structure conversations for action.** Moving the team forward is what these conversations are about. Some small talk is fine but, as a matter of discipline, virtual communication should work from an agenda to ensure that the team addresses essential issues and achieves specified (though modest) goals for each conversation.
- **Integrate productivity tools.** Use a common desktop suite. While conversation is the key, these tools should be readily available and well integrated into the environment."
- **Build a project management system** that provides overall coordination. Include specified subgroups to address different tasks, and a common timeline to bring the right people together at the right time."[14]

The selection of productivity tools and a project management system will require that you or your communication manager ask and answer a series of questions to determine your organization's macro- and micro-communication needs and goals (see Table 5-1). The nature of communication within the team centers on different tasks that participants are asked to complete. According to virtual team expert Lisa Kimball of Group Jazz, this includes but is not limited to the frequency of communication and the degree of interactivity. Different tools raise different sets of questions for managers. Kimball suggests managers ask the following questions in developing a virtual team's communication strategy:

- "What, when (and how much) are we going to communicate?"
- "Where and how will we communicate? (Which media will we use?)"
- "Who will play what roles in the team's communications?"[15]

There is another way to think about the array of communication technologies available to a group. Kimball suggests to ask: Is the focus on information or relationships? Will the target of the communication be confined to private teams or will it be organization-wide (see Table 5-2)? Kimball says that the size of the team should be among the drivers for selecting technology. And team size, she says, is just as significant whether the application is informational or relational. She notes that although information-focused general applications are probably the easiest to get up and running quickly and reap benefits in the short term, the relationship-focused virtual team applications have the potential for the highest leverage to create significant change in the organization, particularly over the long haul.[16]

Kimball cautions that one of the dangers "for virtual teams is that the disconnected feeling of a distributed team sometimes leads to over-reporting as a strategy to give people the feeling of knowing what's going on. Sometimes team members will generate a lot of reporting in order

Table 5-1   Media Selection Issues for Virtual Team Managers

Media	Questions for Team Managers
Computer-supported face-to-face meetings	How does the ability to contribute anonymous input affect the team? How can you continue to test whether consensus as defined by computer processing of input is valid?
Audio conferencing	How can you help participants have a sense of who is present? How can you sense when people have something to say so you can make sure that everyone has a chance to be heard?
War room (perhaps Discovery room would be a better name)	How can you support an engaging conversation about the materials among people who don't access them at the same time? How do you know when it's time to make a decision and when there is closure about it?
Electronic mail	What norms need to be established for things like response time and whether e-mail can be forwarded to others? What norms are important about who gets copied on e-mail messages and whether these are blind copies? How does the style of e-mail messages influence how people feel about the team?
Asynchronous web conferencing	How do you deal with conflict when everyone is participating at different times? What's the virtual equivalent of eye contact? What metaphors will help you help participants create the mental map they need to build a culture that will support the team process?
Document sharing (intranets)	How can you balance the need to access and process large amounts of information with the goal of developing relationships and affective qualities like trust?

Source: Adapted from Kimball, Group Jazz. Used by permission.

to make sure the team leader knows that they are working. This kind of communication creates sludge in the team's arteries. It is a common cause of information overload that can sometimes result in team members avoiding engaging in the communications that actually are important to the team."[17]

To counter this sludge, team members should provide enough information to each other about areas in which their routine work is interdependent to enable them to coordinate, but not so much that it overwhelms the flow of information. Kimball advises that just because we have

Table 5-2   Virtual Teamwork Communication Matrix

	Information	Relationships
Small Work Groups (private)	A web-based shared meeting calendar helps team members schedule meetings. An e-mail list allows project team members to check facts quickly by seeking input from other team members so that they can move on to the next step in their project.	A set of web-based computer conferences serves as a virtual team workspace over a period of weeks or months. An audio-teleconference links team members in real time so that they can come to an agreement around a tricky decision that needs to be made immediately. A desktop video-conference allows a team member to discuss alternative versions of new organization charts with remote team members.
Large Organization Organization-Wide wide Purposes (public)	A web site that includes project updates and organization-wide personnel directories provides information about who is working on different aspects of the change initiative. A Video-teleconference downlink to multiple sites allows top management to send an important message to everyone in the system simultaneously. E-mail list for announcements about large auditorium-style meetings open to everyone allow project teams to make status presentations.	An organization-wide electronic bulletin board allows anyone to post a question about how changes are being implemented and hear from others in the organization about what's going on from their point of view. Facilitated all-hands meetings provide a way for large numbers to provide input and choose to join teams. An electronic suggestion box on a web page provides a way for anyone in the organization to make comments and provide ideas (could be anonymous).

Source: Kimball, Group Jazz, Used by permission.

technology that allows us to exchange and store large amounts of information doesn't mean that we should use it automatically without addressing whether it adds value.[18]

Most important, the team needs to agree on a strategy to manage and coordinate this communication. Kimball suggests choosing a few processes for exchanging critical information and making a commitment about what will be produced by each member of the team.

As the type of work tackled by the virtual team changes, so does the nature of the communication needed to successfully support team members in their work. Kimball notes that when team members notice changes emerging in the work they have been doing, it's critical to make this intelligence available to the team as a whole. "A team that doesn't share this kind of intelligence is less than the sum of its parts, " she says. "The team needs a strategy for scanning and

"Teams whose members fail to share critical information—particularly information about changing conditions—are really less than the sum of their parts."
— Lisa Kimball, Group Jazz ▲

scouting the environment within which they are operating, to observe pattern changes, and to make sure that important things show up on the team's radar screen soon enough when something that has been static begins to change. But it's not enough to simply report the information; it's critical that the whole team have an opportunity to talk about its meaning."[19]

VIRTUAL TEAM LEADERSHIP

The overall success of a virtual team depends largely on the team leader. Kimball points out that this person must be a leader, motivator, and counselor from a distance. Yet she can't possibly make all of the decisions, so she must empower people with specific competencies to make decisions in their areas of core competency. Team members will require encouragement, coaching, and ongoing options for dialogue. The following guidelines may be helpful for virtual team leaders:

- **Start off on the right foot.** Hold an initial face-to-face meeting to establish interdependency among team members. Agree not only on what, when, and how information will be shared but also on how team members will respond to it.
- **Update contact data.** Ensure that all contact information, preferred form of contact (e-mail, voice mail, wireless handheld, or other means) and time availabilities are correct and clear. Post this information on a message board.
- **Agree on frequency.** Establish how often workers must access online information and the response times expected for the different forms of communication.
- **Agree on style and tone.** Define the appropriate uses of online communication tools and tone of communication, including colloquialisms and other borderline communication styles.[20]
- **Work for transparency.** Make the whole project visible to everyone by providing a "line of sight" to the team's goal and the larger organization's goals.
- **Share what you know.** Share knowledge on the basis of information pull from individual members, not a centralized push from the team leader. This can help to transform each individual's personal knowledge into organizational knowledge.[21]
- **Connect occasionally in person.** Remember that virtual teams work, yet few teams are 100 percent virtual. Formative stages, conflict resolution, team building, and rich interactive communication are best done face to face.
- **Build trust.** Acknowledge that if the people you've hired are worthy of trust in the traditional workplace, then they can be trusted to complete tasks in a timely manner offsite.

Kimball thinks that a virtual team manager's mindset must shift in order to be effective in contemporary organizations.[22] To address the challenges and opportunities posed in facilitating the work of distributed teams, the manager's mindset must address different communication techniques for success in working with teams on the web. Virtual team managers who successfully adjust their predispositions to communication in the ways noted in Table 5-3 are most likely to lead successful teams.

Within any virtual team, a communication manager and leader must wear several hats, sometimes separately, sometimes concurrently. And as the goals of a virtual team change, Kimball asserts that communication leaders will find themselves in at least one of the following four roles:

- **Defenders** act as buffers between the team and the rest of the organization. They defend the team against unnecessary and overloading reporting requirements. They also make sure that the team isn't generating excess information.
- **Managers** help the team develop habits to make these processes run smoothly and reliably.
- **Lookouts** are constantly scanning the landscape of the team looking for indicators of problems and changes. Kimball calls this "helicopter management" because of the ability to hover above the fray and then swoop down as needed.
- **Facilitators** ensure collaboration and engagement by all team members. Kimball likens the facilitator role to that of a "producer" who brings together all the key players and makes sure that each is contributing effectively to the collective.[23]

Table 5-3   Mind-Shift Needed to Manage a Virtual Team

Mind Shift From	To
Face to face is the best environment for interaction and anything else is a compromise.	Different kinds of environments can support high-quality interaction. What matters is how you use them.
Collaboration is what happens when teams interact at a fixed time and space.	Collaboration happens in an ongoing, boundaryless way.
Being people-oriented is incompatible with using technology.	Using technology in a people-oriented way is possible and desirable.
When the communication process breaks down, blame the technology.	When the communication process breaks down, evaluate management and interaction strategies, not just the technical tool.
Learning to manage virtual teams is about learning how to use the technology.	Learning to manage virtual teams is about understanding more about teams and the collaboration process.

Source: Kimball, Group Jazz. Used by permission.

Regardless of which role they assume, virtual team leaders operate within a different framework than their office-bound colleagues. David Gould, Department Chair for Information Systems and Technology at the Seattle campus of the University of Phoenix, points out that despite adequate team preparation and technology selection, some elements of virtual teamwork fall short of the traditional, office-based team experience. For instance, Gould found that while team leaders do offer support and coaching to team members, they are less likely to offer individual recognition to team members. Celebrations of virtual team accomplishments also were rare.[24] On the upside," people can be recruited for their competencies, not just physical location; many physical handicaps are not a problem; and expenses associated with travel, lodging, parking, and leasing or owning a building may be reduced and sometimes eliminated. Plus it beats traveling," says Gould.

WHAT DO VIRTUAL TEAMS MEAN FOR YOU?

Are virtual teams the answer for just about any contemporary business problem? Well, obviously not. Some business problems simply demand that team members, co-workers, and colleagues be in the same building—or the same room—at the same time. Some goals demand the kind of collaboration that can be accomplished only with immediate feedback, personal contact, and high-context communication. Most organizations, happily, are set up for just that sort of thing. Everything from socializing to brainstorming can take place within shouting distance, or, perhaps, arms' reach. But is that optimal—or even necessary—for all organizations?

Terry Holbrooke, Group Vice President for Ziff-Davis—an innovative firm that publishes magazines, runs trade shows, and operates an Internet news service—says no. "ZD keeps a significant edge on its competition," she notes, "by operating in multiple time zones 24 hours a day." A project as simple as a press release or feature story might gain several days' lead time on the competition with a virtual team on the job. "My staff in New York will gather some information for me early in the day and pass it to my office in San Francisco. I'll look at it after lunch, organize some of the ideas and craft a few paragraphs, just to get the team going. When I'm headed for home at six o'clock in California, that e-package is headed for our office in Singapore." Holbrooke's English-speaking assistant in Singapore works on the project a bit longer and then passes it on to a staffer in Bombay. If the project needs still more work, she'll forward the package to a woman in London who'll tidy things up before sending it back to Holbrooke in San Francisco. "By the time I'm back in the office the next morning, the project is ready for me to proofread and approve. We've saved two or three days' work with the use of a virtual team." Some of those team members, by the way, she's never met face to face. "I talk with them on the phone. I know their credentials, I know their work, I know their capabilities. I'm not sure I'll ever get to meet some of them."[25]

Whether virtual teams will work for your organization is a question only you and your organizational leadership can answer. Properly organized, properly equipped, and properly supported, however, virtual teams can literally transform the way you do business overnight.

DISCUSSION QUESTIONS

1. What is the greatest problem for members of virtual teams?

2. What are some ways that communication managers can help improve virtual team communication?

3. What are some of the day-to-day challenges facing both communication managers and team members who work virtually?

4. What is the disconnected feeling common to virtual teams, and, if left untreated, how can it undermine team success.

5. What steps can virtual team leaders take to increase the probability of team success?

ENDNOTES

1. J. Lipnack, CEO, Virtual Teams.com. Retrieved June 18, 2001, from *http://www.virtualteams.com/company/press/LiNE%20Zine%20Spring%202001.htm*.
2. B. Bruck. "How Companies Work, Creating Distributed Teams Online," A Caucus Systems Whitepaper. Retrieved May 8, 2000, from *http://www.caucus.com/pdf/howcompanieswork.pdf*.
3. According to the Washington-based International Telework Association & Council. As quoted in "Think of People When Planning Virtual Teams." J. Dash. February 5, 2001. *http://www.computerworld.com*.
4. Lipnack.
5. D. Gould, Campus Department Chair for Information Systems and Technology at the University of Phoenix—Washington (Seattle) Campus. Retrieved July 2, 2001, from *http://www.leader-values.com/Guests/Gould.htm*.
6. Ibid.
7. T. Hoefling. *Managing People for Successful Virtual Teams and Organizations.* (Sterling, VA: Stylus Publishing, 2001).
8. Gould.
9. For more on the relationship between proximity and collaboration, see T. J. Allen, *Managing the Flow of Technology: Technology Transfer and the Dissemination of Technological Information within the R&D Organization* (Cambridge, Mass.: M.I.T. Press, 1977). Data are given in "The Age of the Network," p. 47.
10. Ibid.
11. Gould.
12. Ibid.
13. T. Fairhead and R Lewis. "A Field Study Examining Project Management and Collaborative Software in the Workforce." Mendoza College of Business, University of Notre Dame, 1999.
14. Bruck.
15. L. Kimball, Executive Producer, Group Jazz. Retrieved July 21, 2001, from *http://www.groupjazz.com*. Used with permission.
16. Ibid.
17. Ibid.
18. Ibid.
19. Ibid.
20. T. Hoefling. "The Virtual Workforce of the (Now) Future." Training Directors' Forum, June 10–13, 2001, Las Vegas, Nevada.
21. Kimball. Retrieved June 21, 2001, from *http://www.groupjazz.com*. Used with permission.

22. Kimball. Retrieved June 16, 2001, from *http://www.groupjazz.com*. Used with permission.
23. Kimball. Retrieved June 16, 2001, from *http://www.groupjazz.com*. Used with permission.
24. Gould.
25. T. Holbrooke, personal communication, Arthur W. Page Society Spring Seminar, April 1999, New York Stock Exchange.

6 MEASURING THE VALUE OF E-TECHNOLOGY IN THE WORKPLACE

E-technology is a critical corporate asset for organizations that expect to compete successfully in the fourth economy. And, as with any business asset, measuring outcomes is crucial. To realize e-technology's full value, however, you must know not only what to measure, but how to measure it. The benefits of e-technology should be measured in more than traditional financial metrics, such as ROI (return on investment) or ROE (return on equity), but increasingly, they must be measured in terms of the competitive advantage and market leadership they confer.

Tech Talk ▼

"We may think we're losing when we are actually winning if we don't keep score."
— Mark Samuel, President, IMPAQ
Accountability-Based Consulting
and Training ▲

This chapter proposes that communication managers consider calculating their return on communication investment (RCI) as part of the technology evaluation process. If increasing percentages of the communication budget are allocated to purchase tools to enhance technology—such as cellular telephones or collaboration software—or are allocated to the cost of building and maintaining a corporate portal or intranet, it only makes sense to have some means to independently measure the value delivered by such investments.

Before you can conduct a meaningful assessment, you require an understanding of just what measurable communication value is. While not exhaustive, here is a list of variables that could explain that value.[1]

- Reaction of participants (satisfaction)
- Learning achieved (increased knowledge, improved skills, changed attitudes)
- Implementation of technology over time
- Performance improvements in the job
- Tangible results on business
- Intangible results on business

In evaluating these factors, you should ask specific questions that identify how new technologies have made communication-related tasks more effective. Focus on practical mastery, such as improvement in employee skills, or technology adaptation levels, which are really attitudinal measure. Keep in mind that more than one measure may be needed to calculate an accurate return, as people within the organization are likely to move through levels of skill growth and technology acceptance at varying rates.

These would include transitions from personal awareness of the technology to performance improvement to ongoing effectiveness as new methodologies are implemented. This should lead to personal and organizational transformation as the rates of adaptation climb beyond the rates of non-accepting or untrained employees.[2]

EVALUATING YOUR ORGANIZATIONAL RETURN ON COMMUNICATION INVESTMENT

Evaluating changes that have occurred through communication technology investment—particularly those requiring large investments of cash, space, and staff—will permit management to know how (and whether) those programs have contributed to the business. These changes can also gain support for further investment by ensuring that training and learning processes are improved and that unproductive changes are identified and eliminated. By doing so, your organization can expand on successful programs and build credibility with senior management. It may also be useful to consider your return on communication investment (RCI) not only for start-up and training costs but also for the cost of maintaining your system at peak performance levels. Systems analysts often refer to this under the heading of life cycle costing.

Two issues seem particularly important as you evaluate new technology: first, isolating the new skills you want people to learn and, second, identifying those attitudes that pinpoint whether they've bought into the changes. If you, as a communication manager, can develop techniques for evaluating progress on those two issues, your investment in technology has at least some prospect for success. Jack and Patricia Phillips of the Jack Phillips Center for Research in Salt Lake City encourage managers to consider the following possibilities for evaluation.

1. **Reaction of participants** is a measure of satisfaction with the technology. This "qualitative" measure also can begin to calculate fear and resistance to technology adaptation. Using a Likert scale to evaluate response from one through five (where one equals strongly agree and five equals strongly disagree), you can assess how employee attitudes have changed toward communication technology and its implementation in the workplace. Questions could include:
   a. "I knew that my team would be more efficient once everyone on the team had the same software."
   b. "The ability to work from home using our corporate portal is one of the best aspects of my job."
   c. "I'd gladly sacrifice some privacy to have access to my e-mail from anywhere in the world."

2. **Achieved learning** is a combination measure of increased knowledge and improved skills. You should measure both, since your employees could possess a theoretical understanding of how technology works without actually having completed the training to develop or improve their skill base. These areas could be measured through a combination of quizzes and hands-on exercises. Quizzes administered at least two weeks after the completion of training sessions will help to evaluate long-term knowledge retention among employees.

Placing these quizzes on your new corporate portal will also require that your employees embrace the new technology required to complete the assignment. Peer training may also be helpful. It is certainly an effective means to assess achieved learning—as the process of teaching someone else reinforces both what an employee knows and how well he can apply it.

3. **Implementation of technology** over time helps to account for the "new toy" factor—the feeling that comes with artificially high levels of acceptance. This evaluation is similar to that described for achieved learning but should be administered over longer intervals. This measurement assesses diffusion by recognizing that a new technology must reach critical mass before its effect can be fully recognized.[3] For instance, it took approximately 50 years for the impact of electricity to be felt and measured on a national scale. If only 20 percent of a workforce adapts to a communication technology, it would be hard to argue that their RCI is as sound as an organization with a 60-percent adaptation rate.

4. **Performance improvements in the job** are a measure of technology adaptation, based on the working assumption that communication technology allows employees to become more efficient and more productive. One way to calculate this is to observe changes in employee behavior, such as meeting tighter deadlines for written assignments while maintaining standards for quality. Job promotions, departmental recognition for performance, and positive client feedback also are useful in assessing these factors.

5. **Tangible results on business** measure the standard predictors of organizational success, such as ratios of profits and earnings measured against costs, including capital investments. In addition to these factors, numerous data that support the communication process can be converted to dollar value. These might include
   a. Output-to-contribution (set standard value)
   b. Cost of quality
   c. Employee time (wages)
   d. Historical costs
   e. Resource internal or external experts
   f. External database information
   g. Link-in with other measures
   h. Gain estimates from participants[4]

6. **Intangible results on business** include improvements to an organization's reputation as a front-runner in communication technology, as well as morale boosters to employees who know that they have access to the newest and best technology in the workplace.

REALIZING THE VALUE OF INFORMATION TECHNOLOGY

Another way to evaluate communication technology effectiveness is to divide "return" into an assessment of foundational and innovative activities. As you can see in Figure 6-1, "foundational activities such as increasing organizational effectiveness rely on traditional evaluation methods and quantitative metrics, such as ROI and break-even analysis. For innovative activities such as changing an industry's structure, you should consider more qualitative assessments such as market share, customer satisfaction, and strategic alignment with other business initiatives."[5]

Two practical management exercises include calculating the cost/benefit ratio of an investment and comparing the costs and improvements of old (bricks-and-mortar) methods versus the new electronic methods. You can use cost/benefit ratios with foundational activities such as

Figure 6-1   **Measuring Foundational versus Innovative Activities**

The value spectrum can help both technical and nontechnical executives clarify what a specific investment is intended to achieve and establish the relevant criteria to evaluate its impact.

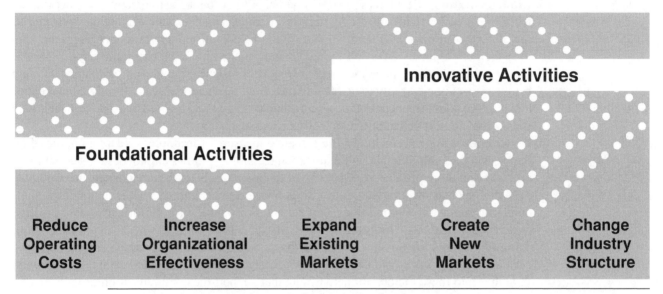

Source: "Beyond the Productivity Paradox: New Views on the Value of Information Technology." Retrieved July 15, 2001, from *http://www-3.ibm.com/e-business/resource/pdf/26516.pdf.*

those we just discussed, as well as sales, hiring, and retention. You should evaluate the cost of the previous method in order to provide a base against which the new e-method can be measured.[6] Categories can include benefits, savings, time, and feedback.

Innovational activities are managed over longer periods of time, much like the expenses associated with research and development. More visionary in nature, these activities require buy-in from the most senior management to ensure long-term support and success.

MANAGING THE MEASUREMENT OF GAINS FROM COMMUNICATION TECHNOLOGY

Before new technology can be properly evaluated, you must manage its use effectively to produce the business returns you want. This means learning how to strategically apply technology to business processes and to assess the results in terms of defined business goals.[7] Clearly, the *implementation* of evaluation is critical to this management process. If your organization mishandles the implementation phase, communication technology managers and users may observe that

- Training and development results are unclear,
- Costs for training and development are unexpected or dramatically higher than anticipated,
- Upper management support for communication training and development is diminishing,
- Requests for cost justifications of new technology and training programs have increased, and
- Skill and attitudinal changes may be out of sync with business needs and goals.[8]

"Look for untapped ways to leverage your technology. When is it not being used, and is there a way to recapture some of that revenue?"

— Bill Brewster, Director of Technology,
Mendoza College of Business Executive
MBA programs, The University of
Notre Dame ▲

One approach to avoiding all this is to implement a life cycle approach to evaluation. This ensures a continuous feedback loop (as opposed to standalone evaluation) that begins when new methodologies or programs are first implemented.[9] This assessment tool could be web-based or handled through focus or feedback groups.

Measurable life cycles include the following stages:

- Definition of the business goal,
- Definition of the communications goal,
- Selection of the technology,
- Training,
- Application,
- Specification of business performance (or activities) with measures inherent in the method,
- Identification of measures from a process that has already occurred,
- Redefinition of business and communication goals as necessary, and
- Rollout of technology on a wider and deeper scale within the organization.

THE BOTTOM LINE

There is little question that companies stand to benefit substantially from e-technology tools and web teaming techniques. The problem has always been how a manager could successfully (and inexpensively) measure the success of new investments in technology. Each of us knows, without exception, two things for sure: First, none of this investment is cheap. The costs of new equipment, smart people, implementation, space, and service agreements are enough to cause bullish, square-jawed CFOs to hyperventilate—to say nothing of the cost of capital itself. Second, the investment you make today isn't good for long. Everything—literally everything—from processing speed to screen resolution to storage capacity will change by the close of business Friday. How do we know what the right investment will be? And how can we know if we're realizing any benefit from the resources we've committed?

Implementing a technology assessment program similar to the one we've just discussed can help. But as you do, think carefully about three basic considerations:

- First, what quantitative measures are most important in other areas of your business? Do you gather data on return on investment and if so, why wouldn't it apply in the case of communication technology?
- Second, what qualitative measures do you worry about elsewhere in your business? Customer satisfaction? Employee quality-of-life measures? Return rates? Product failure rates? Independent satisfaction indices (J. D. Power and Associates rankings, Malcom Baldridge Awards, and more)? If any of those are important to you, it makes good sense to see what effect new communication technology has on them.

- Finally, what's the cost of doing nothing? Are competitors acquiring and implementing new communication technology at a faster rate than you are? Will any of your chief competitors threaten your market share, mind share, brand recognition, corporate reputation, or profitability? If so, can you afford to stand by and allow them to gain an advantage?

Learning to live with new technology isn't all bad. Cool things happen to companies and people who adapt to new ways of living, working, and doing business. Some companies make bad decisions—buying equipment or services they don't really need or technology that won't do what they need it to. Others simply overspend, investing more in a highly transitory system that they should. Getting it right isn't easy.

One way to increase your comfort level with all of this is to raise your tolerance for speed—and for the rate of change in your market space. Things simply will not remain static for long. Markets, methods, and media will occasionally pause to catch their breath, but before long, they charge ahead—whether you're ready or not. Raising your comfort and confidence levels is mostly psychological. Keep reading about what's new, what works, and what's just over the horizon. Test-drive the equipment; see how it works. Lease or rent if you're not really sure. Build performance incentives into the contracts you sign with service providers and equipment vendors. Make sure employees, associates, partners, and allies all understand what your business goals are and what their role will be in achieving them.

The very fact that you've read this far tells us you're ready for the next step.

DISCUSSION QUESTIONS

1. What are some of the variables used to measure the value of communication as enhanced by electronic technology?

2. How will managers know if capital investments in electronic technology supporting communication have really contributed to the company's bottom line?

3. How can managers measure employee satisfaction with electronic technology?

4. How can mangers measure the rate and level of technology adaptation among employees?

5. When calculating a return on your electronic technology investment, what is the difference between foundational activities and innovative activities?

ENDNOTES
1. D. Kirkpatrick. "Evaluating Training Programs: Inside the Four Levels." Presentation at Training Directors' Forum, June 10–13, 2001, Las Vegas, Nevada.
2. L. Russell. "Monitoring Organizational Transformation: A Life Cycle Approach." Presentation at Training Directors' Forum, June 10–13, 2001, Las Vegas, Nevada.
3. "Beyond the Productivity Paradox: New Views on the Value of Information Technology." Retrieved July 8, 2001, from *http://www-3.ibm.com/e-business/resource/pdf/26516.pdf*.
4. J. Phillips and P. P. Phillips. "ROI for the Beginner." Presentation at Training Directors' Forum, June 10–13, 2001, Las Vegas, Nevada.
5. "Beyond the Productivity Paradox: New Views on the Value of Information Technology." Retrieved July 8, 2001, from *http://www-3.ibm.com/e-business/resource/pdf/26516.pdf*.

6. M. W. Mercer. "Measuring the Profit Improvement of Your OD & T&D Efforts." Presentation at Training Directors' Forum, June 10–13, 2001, Las Vegas, Nevada.

7. Ibid.

8. Phillips and Phillips.

9. Russell, op.cit.

A THE E-LEARNING READINESS SCALE*

These simple, easy-to-use questionnaires can provide a quick and relatively accurate assessment of whether your employees or the members of your organization are ready for e-learning. And, once you're sure they are ready, you'll have a simple, direct method of assessing everything from e-learning design to instructional content, delivery, and supplier relationships.

You can use this set of eight instruments to begin gathering the information you'll need to make an investment decision. Please feel free to modify or customize this set of questions for your organization. The questions should be sequenced in the order of greatest importance to you. The most important issues should come first because you don't have time to waste.

There are numerous competitors in the e-learning business. Your task is to sort out those who best suit your needs. By framing your questions in the context of your needs, you can determine quickly if a supplier has the best approach for your organization.

---

*Source: Adapted from D. Woodall, E-Learning Consultant. Retrieved from *http://www.internettime.com/itimegroup/woodall.htm#_Toc484301695.* Used with permission

The E-Learning Readiness Scale

Criteria	Rating (1 = low, 10 = high)
1. You have a large population of learners.	1 2 3 4 5 6 7 8 9 10
2. Learners are dispersed in different geographical locations.	1 2 3 4 5 6 7 8 9 10
3. Most of the learners have access to the Internet or an intranet.	1 2 3 4 5 6 7 8 9 10
4. A wide range of business, technical, and professional skills are needed.	1 2 3 4 5 6 7 8 9 10
5. Training requirements are generally consistent for most of the audience (e.g., Microsoft Office, Lotus Notes, etc.).	1 2 3 4 5 6 7 8 9 10
6. Training is being done now using either CBT, CD-ROM, or LAN.	1 2 3 4 5 6 7 8 9 10
7. You are not strongly rooted to a classroom-only tradition.	1 2 3 4 5 6 7 8 9 10
8. An established, recognized training function already exists.	1 2 3 4 5 6 7 8 9 10
9. There is a strong belief in learning design for individuals.	1 2 3 4 5 6 7 8 9 10
10. There is a long-term commitment to technology.	1 2 3 4 5 6 7 8 9 10
11. Your company intranet is in place and working.	1 2 3 4 5 6 7 8 9 10
12. Some online learning or information tools are in place.	1 2 3 4 5 6 7 8 9 10
13. Help desk receives a high quantity of inquiries because skills are not in place.	1 2 3 4 5 6 7 8 9 10
14. IT group is supportive, has equipment, or will allow external Internet hosting.	1 2 3 4 5 6 7 8 9 10
15. Organization sees an increase in individual skills as a key to business growth within market.	1 2 3 4 5 6 7 8 9 10
16. Management sees a return on the investment or clear strategic advantage for training function.	1 2 3 4 5 6 7 8 9 10
17. Adequate resources (people, equipment, and funding) are available to manage the program.	1 2 3 4 5 6 7 8 9 10
18. Culture is open to e-learning (commitment to lifelong learning).	1 2 3 4 5 6 7 8 9 10
19. The e-learning implementation team has a clear vision.	1 2 3 4 5 6 7 8 9 10
20. Your organization is economically sound and has the budget needed to see the program through for the next 3 to 4 years.	1 2 3 4 5 6 7 8 9 10

ANALYSIS

Once you have completed rating your organization, connect the scores with a line. A pattern will emerge. If the line goes mostly down the right side, then your organization is ready for an e-learning project. If the line is skewed mostly to the left, then you are less prepared for the venture. Before you consider investing in any e-learning project or program, you must first address these readiness issues with your employees or team members.

Section A: E-Learning Design Questions

Rationale

The training delivered by the supplier's courseware must do a good job of teaching the subject matter. Navigation and other course features are important, but once the course interface is understood, the learner is ready for the delivery of the training content in a way that speeds his or her understanding and skills. You are looking for a positive answer from all of the following questions.

1. Are the practice simulations well constructed, allowing the learner to achieve a stated goal in different ways?	Simulations are needed to increase the learner's engagement with the material. Task or goal-based simulation increases learning dramatically.
2. Does the instruction provide a prescribed learning path?	Learning paths focus the learner on the material that is less familiar to him or her.
3. Does the instruction provide certification exam preparation along with a curriculum, related course, and unit tests?	Embedded preparation for exams saves the learner time.
4. Is the instruction built using a strong instructional design methodology (Gagné, Bloom, Piaget, Mager, and others)?	References to known learning experts are helpful in determining the quality of the training materials.
5. Does the supplier have a learning object strategy that is open and allows you to insert your own custom objects?	Open standards for learning objects are important (AICC or LRN).
6. Are the graphics used within the instruction extensive, meaningful, and within context?	Graphics increase the quality of the learning and are extremely useful in conveying the context of the material.
7. Is pre- and post-testing available?	The learner will shorten his or her training with a pre-test and validate his or her learning with a post-test.
8. Is there a final test?	A final test ensures that the learner has completed the training.
9. Does the content contain social stereotypes or prejudices?	If the course does, then it should be rejected.
10. Are the graphical images and vocabulary representative of the target audience?	Without the best presentation, the message may be missed.
11. Can the library be actively played via the Internet and alternatively be downloaded for off-line use?	Since the learner can take the materials from a workplace or home location, both methods are important.
12. Does the instruction contain basic navigation features such as Bookmark, Step Back, Online Notes, Web Links, Index, or Glossary?	The user interface should be friendly and powerful, allowing the learner to control the pace of the learning.

Section B: Instructional Content Questions

Rationale

Without the right content, the training is useless. You should know if the content will be the best material suited for your training requirements. You are looking for a positive answer from all of the following questions, except where noted.

1. Is the content highly rated by subject matter experts?	Content is king when it comes to learning, so it is a good idea to have the course content reviewed by your own subject matter experts.
2. Does the content match the requirements of your training program?	Obviously the content can be excellent, but does it give you what you need for your training program?
3. What is the range of course topics covered in the supplier's catalog?	You should expect a wide range of course topics within the supplier's catalog. This includes technical, desktop, and business skills.
4. If you have global learners, is the course content localized into multiple languages?	Your training requirements may span over many cultures. Having the same course content available to these audiences will be valuable.
5. Is the content jointly developed with the software providers?	This should mean that the course content is current and up to date. *See the list below for a sampling of providers.
6. Do the software providers use these courses internally for their own staff?	If the providers use the course materials themselves, then it is a very good indication that they see the quality of the content.
7. Does the content use realistic, business-like scenarios?	This ensures that the learner can quickly use the skills within a real business situation.
8. Is the content chunked into small enough units to allow the learner to learn quickly?	If the content is broken up into small units, the learner can take the course in a shorter period of time.
9. Can learners preview courses from your web sites without being charged?	One of the best ways to preview a course is to download from the supplier's web site.
10. Is the content accurate and up to date?	Obviously you need to verify the currency of the content.

*Sample list of software providers:

Microsoft	Lotus	Intel	SkillScape
Novell	SAP	Informix	Javasoft Consortium
Oracle	CISCO	Tibco	Rational Software
Netscape	Project Management	Macromedia	
Sybase Powersoft	Institute	Marimba	
IBM	CompTIA	RealNetworks	

Section C: E-Learning Features Questions

Rationale

The balance e-learning brings to training includes the personalized, collaborative, and mentoring elements. It is with these elements that the learner moves beyond the asynchronous environment to a rich synchronous one that allows him or her to communicate with peers, instructors, and experts. This support gives the learner the opportunity to enrich and construct his or her own learning. You are looking for a positive answer from all of the following questions, except where noted.

1. Does the e-learning interface provide personalized content for the individual learner?	Personalization connects the learner to the learning. It makes it unique for the learner, and this increases the learner's motivation to learn.
2. Is the learner given the capability to build a prescribed learning path based on a pre-assessment test?	Building the personal plan eliminates topics the learner already knows or wishes to skip over, thereby reducing time.
3. Is exam preparation software available for industry certification programs?	Having the ability to prepare for the exam in advance will increase the likelihood of passing the exam.
4. Does the interface provide links from the course to technical documents, whitepapers, articles, case studies, and so on?	Having access to current information about the subject is essential to the learner staying current.
5. Is there an available library (nonmarketing) of news, features, articles, and books on IT and business skills content?	Resources like these will keep the learner aware of trends in his or her career and industry.
6. Are industry video seminars integrated with chats (both live and archived) available from the supplier?	Being able to extract seminars online will increase the learner's understanding of the topic.
7. Does the learning include lab exercises?	Learning is mastered by doing the tasks. Doing them in labs is a good way to support the learner.
8. Are hosted expert-led forums and chats available?	Collaboration is key to the learner constructing his or her own learning.
9. Are hosted discussion threads available?	Ditto above.

10. Are the following features available to you on a private basis? (All of the following functions provide your learners with essential information about your organization.)

- An organizational resource page for internal contacts, internal training news, information, surveys, evaluations, and so on
- A corporate chat room
- A corporate discussion thread
- A corporate resources page with links to specified Internet/intranet sites
- An infrastructure for adding specific content, courseware, publications, and so on

(*continues*)

Section C: E-Learning Features Questions (continued)

11. Does the learner have the capability to customize individual learning paths?	Customization is a very powerful element of e-learning because it allows the learner to build his or her own plan, and this, in turn, builds ownership.
12. Is there an up-to-date course catalog?	Since the learner's needs grow, resources should be made available.
13. Is there an up-to-date schedule of events, shows, and conferences?	You want access to current information that may be useful to your learner.

Section D: Mentoring Services Questions

Rationale	
Mentoring provides the learner with both expert advice and support. In many cases the learner will benefit from the supportive environment created by the mentor much in the same way as having an instructor. You are looking for a positive answer from all of the following questions, except where noted.	
1. Does the supplier provide proactive mentoring (e.g., daily e-mails from learning advisors)?	As in a classroom environment, proactive support by the instructor can motivate the learner to stay on track with his or her learning plan.
2. Does the supplier provide reactive mentoring (e.g., learning advisor chats)?	This method of using chat rooms can provide the learner with just-in-time information or expertise.
3. Are the mentoring learning advisors certified in the subjects they mentor?	Obviously the best mentors are the ones with experience and commitment. Certification is a primary way to confirm their skills and experience.
4. What is the availability to the learning advisors?	Having the advisor available when your learner needs her is essential for learner support. Check into the hours of availability. The more the better.
5. What topic areas are covered by the learning advisors?	Their topics must cover your needs.
6. Is the mentoring developed with the supplier's courseware?	If they do, then this is the best match for your learners.
7. Is the supplier's courseware actually used by the learning advisors?	Mentoring is best if it is blended with the use of the supplier's courses; check to be sure that this is being done.
8. What are the guaranteed and actual response times of the learning advisors?	You should expect a quick turnaround for the service you are buying.

Section E: Supplier Support Questions

Rationale

Implementing an e-learning environment will require support from the supplier. In a true partnership, the supplier will work with your organization to make your e-learning program a success. You are looking for a positive answer from all of the following questions, except where noted.

1. What is the size of the supplier's support organization (technical and learning)?	The larger the better. Compare the staff size and experience levels with the nearest competitive supplier.
2. Will the supplier provide onsite support to assist you with your e-learning program?	Being there is a big asset for your organization. Be sure to confirm that they will be around throughout your program.
3. Is there a professional services group to assist with custom integration and development?	Customizing your program may be necessary so having consulting support from the same supplier can save time and money.
4. How responsive is their toll-free technical and e-mail support?	It is best if their support is available 24/7. One way to check them out is to call the service at a very early time in the morning, say 4:00 A.M.

Section F: Deployment System Questions

Rationale

Tracking the learner's progress is essential to the success of the e-learning program. This oversight function is not being done to show Big Brother control but to determine if the program is truly effective and whether it is bringing about the business results. You are looking for a positive answer from all of the following questions, except where noted.

1. Does the supplier provide a learner management system (LMS) to launch and track the learners' progress?	All e-learning suppliers must provide a system that does this since there is no other choice when launching and tracking training events.
2. Does the LMS work equally as well on the Internet and your intranet?	This is an important feature since the learner may be accessing training materials from different locations.
3. Is the LMS rich in functions and easy to use? (E.g., can you add and modify courses, events, and curricula for individuals or groups? Are you allowed to export or import data to and from the LMS?)	The richer the LMS, the better it is for you and your organization. There are several key functions that you should review in detail.
4. Can individual and group reports (usage, scores, downloads) be customized?	The ability to obtain usage information is essential to LMS. Without this customization function, much of the richness of the LMS is lost.
5. Does the supplier provide a qualified hosted provider?	Be sure to ask for references about the quality of technical and people resources at the host site.
6. What is the service history for the provider in terms of transactions and uptime?	Ask for a service history from customers similar to those having your requirements.
7. Can the LMS launch and track other supplier courses?	This capability means the LMS is open and not restricted to only one supplier.
8. Is the supplier committed to open system standards (AICC, LRN, IEEE, or IMS)?	Look for evidence of the supplier's participation in industry groups that are committed to building open standards; it shows that they are concerned about the industry.
9. What is the total installed size of the instruction on the hard drive?	Course size is important when downloading or when managing hard disk space. Look for those that are consistently less than 15 megabytes.
10. Will the instruction perform well using a 28.8K modem?	Most learners will have this modem speed when away from their office locations.
11. Does the instruction library have a consistent course interface when delivered via Internet, intranet, or CD-ROM?	Once the learner has mastered the interface, then his or her ability to learn will increase.

Section G: Supplier Credentials Questions

Rationale	
The financial and development qualities of the supplier are proof of their true commitment and vision to their customers and the training industry.	
1. When was your company founded? Have you changed your name? Why?	The longer they have been in the business, the better. Look for the strength of their financial position, leadership, and vision.
2. How many clients do you have currently?	The more customers, the better. It shows that you can get a reference check on the supplier. Also look into the loyalty of their customer base and if any left the supplier but later came back.
3. Can you describe your principal product in terms that my boss would understand?	Look for a simple statement of what they supply. A business-like statement about how they will save you money is a good answer.
4. Does your company supply a full e-learning solution (content, technology, and service)?	Knowing if the supplier has the full range of expertise to be an e-learning partner is key. All of these components are needed to supply you will a full range of e-learning solutions.
5. What is the number of higher education clients (colleges and universities) using this supplier?	Great question even if you are not in this group. Education customers look at the instructional quality of the products along with the flexibility of delivery and use.
6. Who do you consider to be your major competitors?	They should give you two or more names and strictly avoid any negative selling comments about their competition.
7. In what part of the country or in the world do you do business?	The more locations the better, particularly if your organization has global learners.
8. Has the supplier shown sustained revenue, profit, and growth within the training industry?	If the supplier has been in the training business for any length of time, they must show constant growth or there could be something wrong.
9. How much (as an amount and percentage) does the supplier reinvest into their product development?	A good rule of thumb is at least 15 percent of gross revenue. Without a significant investment the supplier is taking a risk of not being prepared for your future training needs. Spending that type of money usually confirms their commitment.)
10. How many course titles does the supplier have available?	While the number may vary, the total library of courses does show the amount of training resources available to you. Having over 1,000 courses shows a very significant investment in development.

(continues)

Section G: Supplier Credentials Questions (continued)

11. What percentage of the course titles is currently available via the Internet?	Look at how many total courses are available versus how many are available via the Internet. The difference is usually made up of out-of-date courses.
12. Is the supplier's product development staff residing in-house or are they outsourced?	In-house is good since there should be consistent quality and content development. Outsourced courses tend to vary in quality and content depth. The larger the staff, the better. Be sure to compare with the supplier's closest competitor.
13. What awards has the supplier won for the quality of their learning products and services?	They didn't need to win every award. Look at the kind of awards they have won in order to determine if others within the training industry believe their products to be of value too.

B SELECT BIBLIOGRAPHY

ASTD Learning Circuits. *http://www.learningcircuits.org*.

Allen, T. J. *Managing the Flow of Technology: Technology Transfer and the Dissemination of Technological Information within the R&D Organization*. Cambridge, Massachusetts: MIT Press, 1977.

Alexander, S. "Virtual Teams Going Global," *InfoWorld*, November 10, 2000. *http://www.infoworld.com/articles*.

Berman, K. "Business Literacy: Training That Transforms Employees in Business People," *Training Directors' Forum*, June 10–13, 2001, Las Vegas, Nevada.

"Beyond the Productivity Paradox: New Views on the Value of Information Technology," IBM Corporation. *http://www-3.ibm.com/e-business/resource*.

Browning, J., and S. Reiss. "Encyclopedia for the New Economy," *Wired Digital*. *http://hotwired.lycos.com*.

Bruck, B. "How Companies Work: Creating Distributed Teams Online," a Caucus Consortium Whitepaper, May 2000. *http://www.caucus.com*.

Carns, A. "Those Bawdy E-Mails Were Good for a Laugh—Until the Axe Fell," *Wall Street Journal*, February 4, 2000, pp. A1, A8.

Cohen, S. G., C. B. Gibson, A. Levenson, A. Raven. "Virtual Teams Project: Creating Conditions for Effective Virtual Teams," The University of Southern California. *http://www.marshall.usc.edu/ceo/vt/*.

"Collocation and Effective Teamwork: Experts Differ on Whether Physical Proximity Is Mission Critical," *PDBPR*, October 1996. Available online at: *http://www.managementroundtable.com/PDBPR/collocation*.

Cross, J. "Research on the Future of Learning and Business," InternetTime Group, Berkeley, California. *http://www.internettime.com*.

Dash, J. "Think of People When Planning Virtual Teams," February 5, 2001. *http://www.computerworld.com*.

The E-Learning Hub. *http://www.e-learninghub.com.*

The E-Learning Post. *http://www.elearningpost.com.*

The E-Learning Research Center. *http://www.cio.com/research/elearning.*

E-Learning and The European Commission. *http://europa.eu.int/comm/education/elearning.*

E-Learning Magazine. *http://www.elearningmag.com.*

El-Shinnawy, M. and Markus, M. L. (1997). "The Poverty of Media Richness Theory: Explaining People's Choice of Electronic Mail vs. Voice Mail," *International Journal of Human-Computer Studies*, 46, 443–467.

Fairhead, T., and R. Lewis. "A Field Study Examining Project Management and Collaborative Software in the Workforce," College of Business, University of Notre Dame, 1999.

Fathom.com. *http://www.fathom.com.*

Finholt, T., and Sproull, L. S. (1990). "Electronic Groups at Work," *Organization Science*, 1(1), 41–64.

Fullerton, K. "E-Learning Communities: The Missing Link." *Training Directors' Forum*, June 10–13, 2001, Las Vegas, Nevada.

Gould, David. *Virtual Organization. http://www.seanet.com/~daveg.*

Guernsey, L. "You've Got Inappropriate Mail," *The New York Times*, April 5, 2000, pp. C1, C10.

Gundry, J. "The Human Factor: Psychological Factors of M-Work," June 2001. *http://www.knowab.co.uk/wbwmwork.html.*

Gundry, J. "Information and E-Mail Overload," May 2002. *http://www.knowab.co.uk/wbwload.html.*

Hoefling, T. *Managing People for Successful Virtual Teams and Organizations.* Sterling, Virginia: Stylus Publishing, 2001.

Hoefling, T. "The Virtual Workforce of the (Now) Future." *Training Directors' Forum*, June 10–13, 2001, Las Vegas, Nevada.

Hughes, B., and R. Park. "Creating Expertise through Cognitive Task Simulations." *Training Directors' Forum*, June 10–13, 2001, Las Vegas, Nevada.

"IDC Envisions a Time When Majority of Internet Access Will Be Through Wireless Devices," IDC Corporate Press Release. *http://www.idc.com/communications/press.*

"Is M-Commerce Hype Unrealistic?" Cahners' In-Stat Group. *http://www.instat.com/rh/wirelessweek.*

Jarvenapp, S. L., and D. E. Leidner. "Communication and Trust in Global Virtual Teams." *http://www.ascusc.org/jcmc/vol3/issue4/jarvenpaa.html.*

Kirkpatrick, D. "Evaluating Training Programs: Inside the Four Levels." *Training Directors' Forum*, June 10–13, 2001, Las Vegas, Nevada.

Knowledge Ability: Working by Wire, "White Papers, Articles, and Free Materials." *http://www.knowab.co.uk/wbwpapers.*

Kumar, R. L. "Understanding the Value of Information Technology Enabled Responsiveness." Belk College of Business Administration, University of North Carolina at Charlotte. *http://is.twi.tudelft.nl/ejise/vol1/issue1/paper1/paper.html.*

Lipnack, J. "Virtual Teams: Creating the Future." An online essay available at: *http://www.ncpl.org/members/archives/virtual_teams.htm.*

Lipnack, J, and J. Stamps. *Virtual Teams: Reaching Across Space, Time, and Organizations with Technology.* New York: John Wiley, 1997.

LiveLink Virtual Teams. *http://www.virtualteams.com.*

Mercer, M. W. "Measuring the Profit Improvement of Your OD & T&D Efforts." *Training Directors' Forum*, June 10–13, 2001, Las Vegas, Nevada.

Mohrman. S., S. Cohen, and A. Mohrman. *Designing Team-Based Organizations: New Forms for Knowledge Work*, Jossey-Bass Publishers, 1995.

Moxley, J. "Getting Past the Gatekeepers: Managing the Transition to Online Learning," *Training Directors' Forum*, June 10–13, 2001, Las Vegas, Nevada.

The National Educational Technology Plan, United States Department of Education. Washington, D.C., December 2000. *http://www.ed.gov/Technology/elearning/e-learning.*

O'Driscoll, T. "Push, Pull, Connect, Ignore: What Is the Optimal e-Learning Strategy?" *Training Directors' Forum*, June 10–13, 2001, Las Vegas, Nevada.

Olian, J., and N. Pal. "e-Technology as a Tool for Change and Process Improvement." *Penn State Quality Expo 2001*, April 12, 2001. *http://www.psu.edu/president/cqi/events/archives.*

Parkes, E. R. "Why Online Learners Drop Out and What to Do About It." *Training Directors' Forum*, June 10–13, 2001, Las Vegas, Nevada.

Phillips, J. and P. P. Phillips. "ROI for the Beginner." *Training Directors' Forum*, June 10–13, 2001, Las Vegas, Nevada.

Russell, L. "Monitoring Organizational Transofrmation: A Life Cycle Appraoch." *Training Directors' Forum*, June 10–13, 2001.

Schrage, M. "The Relationship Revolution," The Merrill Lynch Forum. *http://www.ml.com.*

Shaw, G. (1993). "The Shape of our Field: Business Communication as a Hybrid Discipline." *Journal of Business Communication*, 30, 297–312.

Smith, P. "Want Virtual Results? Use a Virtual Team." *PDBPR*, January 2000. Available online at *http://www.managementroundtable.com/PDBPR/Preston_virtual_teams.*

Strauss, R. "You've Got Maelstrom," *The New York Times*, July 5, 2001, p. D1.

Sullivan B. "Study: One-Third of Workers Watched," MSNBC News, July 7, 2001.

Townsend, A. M., S. M. DeMarie, and A. R. Hendrickson. "Virtual Teams: Technology and the Workplace of the Future." *Academy of Management Executive*, August 1998, Vol. 12, No. 3, pp. 17–29.

Vogt, E. "Professional Learning Communities: The Key to Success in the New Economy," *Training Directors' Forum*, June 10–13, Las Vegas, Nevada.

"A Wireless World Awaits: Nine Moves That Mobilize Business," IBM Corporation. *http://www-3.ibm.com/communications/press.*

York, T. "Invasion of Privacy? E-mail Monitoring Is on the Rise." *http://www.informationweek.com.*

INDEX